Python for Algorithmic Trading

Mastering Strategies for Consistent Profits

J.P.Morgan

3

Copyright © 2024 by J.P.Morgan

All rights reserved. No part of this book may be used or reproduced in any form whatsoever without written permission except in the case of brief quotations in critical articles or reviews.

Printed in the United States of America.

For more information, or to book an event, contact :

Book design by J.P.Morgan
Cover design by J.P.Morgan

Disclaimer

The information provided in this book, *"Python for Algorithmic Trading: Mastering Strategies for Consistent Profits"* **by J.P. Morgan**, is intended for educational and informational purposes only.

Readers should understand that trading in financial markets involves significant risk and it is possible to lose some or all of your investment. The strategies and techniques discussed in this book are based on the author's research and experience.

Before making any investment decisions, readers are strongly encouraged to seek advice from a qualified financial advisor or professional. The author and publisher disclaim any liability for any direct, indirect, or consequential loss or damage incurred by the reader as a result of applying the information presented in this book.

Introduction

Welcome to *"**Python for Algorithmic Trading: Mastering Strategies for Consistent Profits**"*, your definitive guide to transforming trading ideas into reality with the power of Python. In the fast-paced world of financial markets, the ability to develop and deploy algorithmic trading strategies is a game-changer, offering the potential for increased efficiency, reduced risk, and ultimately, consistent profits.

This book is tailored for Python programmers, web developers, trading enthusiasts, and finance professionals who are eager to delve into the exciting realm of algorithmic trading. Whether you are a seasoned trader looking to automate your strategies or a programmer seeking to apply your coding skills to the financial markets, this book provides the tools and knowledge you need to succeed.

Throughout these pages, you will embark on a comprehensive journey, beginning with the fundamentals of algorithmic trading and moving through to the advanced techniques that can set you apart from the competition. You'll learn how to harness the capabilities of Python's powerful libraries—such as Pandas, NumPy, and Scikit-Learn—to build, test, and deploy trading algorithms that are both robust and profitable.

We start by laying a solid foundation, introducing you to the essential concepts of financial markets, trading strategies, and algorithmic thinking. From there, we dive into the practical application of Python, guiding you through the process of data collection, cleaning, and analysis. You will discover how to develop strategies based on technical indicators, backtest your models to ensure their effectiveness, and implement machine learning techniques to enhance your trading decisions.

Each chapter is designed to build on the previous one, providing you with a step-by-step roadmap to mastering algorithmic trading. Along the way, you'll find hands-on examples, code snippets, and practical exercises that reinforce your learning and help you apply the concepts to real-world scenarios. By the end of this book, you will not only have a deep understanding of algorithmic trading but also a portfolio of strategies ready to deploy in the markets.

But this book is more than just a technical manual; it's a call to action. In an era where data and technology drive financial success, mastering algorithmic trading is not just an advantage—it's a necessity. By leveraging Python, you can automate your trading, reduce the impact of human emotions, and achieve a level of precision that manual trading simply cannot match.

Chapter 1: Python for Algorithmic Trading

Python has become one of the most popular programming languages in the world, and its versatility and simplicity make it an excellent choice for algorithmic trading. Algorithmic trading involves using computer algorithms to make trading decisions in financial markets. These algorithms can analyze large amounts of data and execute trades at high speeds, making them ideal for taking advantage of market inefficiencies and opportunities.

Python's popularity in algorithmic trading is due to several key factors. First, Python is easy to learn and use, making it accessible to traders with varying levels of programming experience. Its simple syntax and readability make it a great choice for beginners, while its powerful features and libraries make it a favorite among experienced programmers.

Python also has a large and active community of developers, which means there are plenty of resources available for traders looking to learn more about algorithmic trading in Python. There are numerous online tutorials, forums, and courses dedicated to using Python for algorithmic trading, making it easy to find help and support when needed.

One of the main reasons Python is so popular in algorithmic trading is its extensive library of tools and packages. Python's standard library includes modules for data manipulation, mathematical calculations, and file handling, making it easy to work with financial data and execute trading strategies. In addition, there are several third- party libraries specifically designed for algorithmic trading, such as Pandas, NumPy, and Matplotlib, which provide additional functionality and tools for analyzing and visualizing data.

Another key advantage of using Python for algorithmic trading is its compatibility with other programming languages and platforms. Python can be easily integrated with other languages like C++ and Java, as well as trading platforms like MetaTrader and Interactive Brokers, allowing traders to develop and execute their strategies across multiple platforms.

In addition to its technical capabilities, Python also offers a number of practical benefits for algorithmic trading. Its open-source nature means that it is free to use and distribute, making it an affordable option for traders looking to develop their own trading systems. Python is also platform-independent, meaning that it can run on any operating system, making it a flexible choice for traders who work across multiple devices.

Overall, Python is an excellent choice for algorithmic trading due to its simplicity, versatility, and extensive library of tools and packages. Whether you are a beginner looking to learn the basics of algorithmic trading or an experienced trader looking to develop advanced trading strategies, Python has everything you need to succeed in the world of algorithmic trading.

Understanding Algorithmic Trading

Algorithmic trading, also known as algo trading, is a method of executing trades using automated pre-programmed trading instructions. These instructions are based on various factors such as price, timing, and volume, and are designed to generate profits at a speed and frequency that is impossible for a human trader to achieve. Algorithmic trading has become increasingly popular in recent years, as it allows traders to execute trades quickly and efficiently, while also minimizing human error and emotion.

The main goal of algorithmic trading is to generate profits by taking advantage of small price discrepancies in the market. These discrepancies can occur due to a variety of factors, such as market inefficiencies, news events, or changes in supply and demand. By using algorithms to analyze market data and execute trades automatically, algo traders can capitalize on these opportunities and generate consistent profits over time.

There are several different types of algorithms that can be used in algorithmic trading. Some algorithms are designed to execute trades based on technical analysis, while others use fundamental analysis or a combination of both. Technical analysis algorithms use mathematical formulas and historical price data to predict future price movements, while fundamental analysis algorithms analyze economic data and news events to make trading decisions.

11

One of the key advantages of algorithmic trading is its speed and efficiency. Since trades are executed automatically by computer programs, algo traders can react to market changes in a matter of milliseconds, far faster than any human trader could. This speed allows algo traders to take advantage of short-term price movements and execute trades at the most favorable prices.

Another advantage of algorithmic trading is its ability to remove human emotion from the trading process. Human traders are often influenced by fear, greed, and other emotions, which can lead to poor decision-making and inconsistent results. By using automated trading algorithms, traders can eliminate these emotional biases and stick to a predetermined trading plan, leading to more consistent profits over time.

Despite its many advantages, algorithmic trading also comes with some risks and challenges. One of the main risks of algo trading is the potential for technical glitches or malfunctions. Since trades are executed automatically by computer programs, there is always a risk that something could go wrong, leading to unexpected losses. To mitigate this risk, algo traders must constantly monitor their algorithms and be prepared to intervene if necessary.

Another challenge of algorithmic trading is the need for sophisticated technology and infrastructure. Algo traders must have access to fast and reliable internet connections, powerful computers, and advanced trading software in order to execute trades quickly and efficiently. This can be costly and time-consuming to set up, especially for individual traders or small firms.

Despite these challenges, algorithmic trading continues to grow in popularity, as more and more traders recognize the benefits of automated trading. In fact, algorithmic trading now accounts for a significant portion of all trades in the financial markets, with some estimates suggesting that up to 80% of all trades are now executed by algorithms.

In addition to its popularity in traditional financial markets, algorithmic trading is also gaining traction in other industries, such as cryptocurrency trading. Cryptocurrencies are highly volatile assets that can experience rapid price fluctuations, making them ideal for algorithmic trading strategies. Many crypto traders are now using automated trading algorithms to capitalize on these price movements and generate profits in the highly competitive crypto market.

Overall, algorithmic trading is a powerful tool that can help traders generate consistent profits by taking advantage of market inefficiencies and price discrepancies. By using automated trading algorithms, traders can execute trades quickly and efficiently, while also minimizing human error and emotion. While there are risks and challenges associated with algo trading, the potential rewards are significant, making it a valuable tool for traders looking to maximize their profits in today's fast-paced financial markets.

Advantages of using Python for Algorithmic Trading

Python has become one of the most popular programming languages in the world, and for good reason. Its simplicity, versatility, and ease of use make it an ideal choice for a wide range of applications, including algorithmic trading. In this article, we will explore some of the advantages of using Python for algorithmic trading.

Easy to learn and use

One of the biggest advantages of Python is its simplicity and readability. The syntax of Python is clean and easy to understand, making it a great choice for beginners and experienced programmers alike. This means that traders can quickly and easily develop and implement trading algorithms without having to spend a lot of time learning a new programming language.

Extensive libraries and tools

Python has a vast ecosystem of libraries and tools that make it easy to implement complex trading algorithms. Some of the most popular libraries for algorithmic trading in Python include NumPy, pandas, and scikit-learn. These libraries provide powerful tools for data analysis, machine learning, and statistical modeling, making it easy to develop sophisticated trading strategies.

High performance

Despite its simplicity, Python is a high-performance language that can handle large amounts of data and complex calculations. The language is also highly scalable, making it suitable for both small-scale and large-scale trading operations. Python's performance can be further enhanced by using tools such as Cython, which allows developers to write C extensions for Python code.

Cross-platform compatibility

Python is a cross-platform language, meaning that trading algorithms developed in Python can be run on any operating system. This makes it easy to deploy algorithms on different trading platforms and ensures that they can be accessed by traders using different devices. Python's cross-platform compatibility also makes it easy to collaborate with other developers and share trading strategies.

Community support

Python has a large and active community of developers who are constantly creating new libraries, tools, and resources for algorithmic trading. This means that traders can easily find help and support when developing their trading algorithms, as well as access to a wealth of knowledge and expertise. The Python community is also known for its inclusivity and willingness to help others, making it a welcoming and supportive environment for traders of all skill levels.

Integration with trading platforms
Python can be easily integrated with a wide range of trading platforms and APIs, making it easy to access real-

time market data and execute trades. Many popular trading platforms, such as Interactive Brokers and MetaTrader, provide APIs that allow developers to connect their Python algorithms directly to the platform. This seamless integration makes it easy to automate trading strategies and execute trades with minimal latency.

Backtesting and optimization

Python provides powerful tools for backtesting and optimizing trading strategies, allowing traders to test their algorithms on historical data before deploying them in real-time. Libraries such as backtrader and zipline provide easy-to-use frameworks for backtesting and optimizing trading strategies, making it easy to evaluate the performance of different algorithms and make informed decisions about which strategies to deploy.

Machine learning and AI capabilities

Python is well-suited for developing machine learning and artificial intelligence algorithms, making it an ideal choice for traders looking to incorporate these technologies into their trading strategies. Libraries such as TensorFlow and scikit-learn provide powerful tools for developing and implementing machine learning models, allowing traders to build predictive models that can analyze market data and make informed trading decisions.

Python is an excellent choice for algorithmic trading due to its simplicity, versatility, and ease of use. The language's extensive libraries and tools make it easy to implement complex trading algorithms, while its high performance and cross-platform compatibility ensure that algorithms can be deployed on any trading platform.

The active Python community provides support and resources for traders of all skill levels, making it easy to develop, test, and optimize trading strategies. With its machine learning and AI capabilities, Python is well-suited for developing advanced trading algorithms that can analyze market data and make informed trading decisions. Overall, Python is a powerful and flexible language that is well-suited for algorithmic trading in today's fast-paced financial markets.

Chapter 2: Setting Up Your Python Environment

Python is a popular programming language that is widely used for various applications, such as web development, data analysis, artificial intelligence, and more. In order to start writing and running Python code, you need to set up your Python environment. This chapter will guide you through the process of setting up your Python environment on your computer.

Installing Python

The first step in setting up your Python environment is to install Python on your computer. Python is available for download from the official Python website (https://www.python.org/). The website provides installers for Windows, macOS, and Linux, so make sure to download the appropriate installer for your operating system.

Once you have downloaded the installer, run it and follow the on-screen instructions to install Python on your computer. During the installation process, you will have the option to add Python to your system PATH, which allows you to run Python from the command line. Make sure to check this option to make it easier to run Python scripts from any directory on your computer.

After the installation is complete, you can verify that Python is installed correctly by opening a command

18

prompt or terminal and typing "python --version". This command should display the version of Python that is installed on your computer.

Using a Code Editor

While you can write Python code in any text editor, using a dedicated code editor can make your coding experience more efficient and enjoyable. There are several code editors available for Python, such as Visual Studio Code, PyCharm, Atom, and Sublime Text.

Visual Studio Code is a popular choice among Python developers due to its versatility, ease of use, and extensive library of extensions. PyCharm is another great option that offers advanced features for Python development, such as code completion, debugging, and version control integration.

Choose a code editor that suits your preferences and install it on your computer. Once you have installed the code editor, you can start writing and running Python code in a more organized and efficient manner.

Setting Up a Virtual Environment

A virtual environment is a self-contained directory that contains a specific version of Python and any packages or libraries that you need for your project. Using virtual environments allows you to isolate your project dependencies and avoid conflicts with other projects on your computer.

To create a virtual environment, open a command prompt or terminal and navigate to the directory where you want to create the virtual environment. Then, run the following command to create a new virtual environment:

```
` ` `

python -m venv myenv


` ` `
```

Replace "myenv" with the name of your virtual environment. This command will create a new directory called "myenv" that contains a copy of the Python interpreter and the standard library.

To activate the virtual environment, run the following command:

On Windows:
```
` ` ` myenv\Scripts\activate
` ` `
```

On macOS and Linux:
```
` ` `

source myenv/bin/activate
` ` `
```

Once the virtual environment is activated, you can install any packages or libraries that you need for your project using the pip package manager. For example, to install the requests library, run the following command:

```
```

pip install requests
```
```

Running Python Scripts

Now that you have set up your Python environment, you can start writing and running Python scripts. Open your code editor and create a new Python file with a ".py" extension. Write your Python code in the file and save it.

To run the Python script, open a command prompt or terminal and navigate to the directory where the script is located. Then, run the following command:

```
```

python script.py
```
```

Replace "script.py" with the name of your Python file. This command will execute the Python script and display the output in the command prompt or terminal.

Conclusion

Setting up your Python environment is an essential step in starting your Python programming journey. By installing Python, using a code editor, setting up a virtual environment, and running Python scripts, you can create and run Python code efficiently on your computer.

In the next chapter, we will explore the basics of Python programming, including data types, variables, operators, and control structures.

Installing Python and Essential Libraries for Algorithmic Trading

Python is a versatile programming language that has become increasingly popular in the field of algorithmic trading. With its simplicity and flexibility, Python has become the language of choice for many traders and developers looking to create and implement trading algorithms.

In this article, we will guide you through the process of installing Python and essential libraries for algorithmic trading. By the end of this guide, you will have a fully functional Python environment ready to start building and testing your trading strategies.

Step 1: Installing Python

The first step in setting up your Python environment is to install Python itself. Python is an open-source programming language, which means that it can be freely downloaded and installed on any operating system.

To install Python, simply visit the official Python website at www.python.org and download the latest version of Python for your operating system. The installation process is straightforward and typically involves running an installer and following the on-screen instructions.

Once Python is installed, you can verify that it has been installed correctly by opening a command prompt or terminal window and typing "python --version". This command should display the version of Python that you have installed on your system.

Step 2: Installing Essential Libraries

In addition to Python itself, there are several essential libraries that you will need to install in order to build and test trading algorithms. These libraries provide the necessary tools and functionality for working with financial data, backtesting strategies, and executing trades.

One of the most important libraries for algorithmic trading is NumPy, which is a powerful library for working with numerical data in Python. NumPy provides support for large arrays and matrices, as well as a wide range of mathematical functions that are essential for building trading algorithms.

To install NumPy, you can use the Python package manager pip by running the following command in your command prompt or terminal window:

```
```

pip install numpy
```
```

Another essential library for algorithmic trading is pandas, which is a data manipulation library that provides tools for working with time series data, such as stock prices and trading volumes. Pandas makes it easy to load, clean, and analyze financial data, making it an indispensable tool for algorithmic traders.

To install pandas, you can use pip by running the following command:

```
```
```

```
pip install pandas
```
```
```

In addition to NumPy and pandas, there are several other libraries that you may find useful for algorithmic trading, such as matplotlib for plotting charts, scikit-learn for machine learning, and TA-Lib for technical analysis. You can install these libraries using pip in a similar manner to NumPy and pandas.

Step 3: Setting Up Your Development Environment

Once you have installed Python and essential libraries, you can start setting up your development environment for algorithmic trading. There are several popular integrated development environments (IDEs) that you can use for Python development, such as PyCharm, Visual Studio Code, and Jupyter Notebook.

PyCharm is a powerful IDE that provides advanced features for Python development, such as code completion, debugging, and version control integration. Visual Studio Code is a lightweight and versatile code editor that is well-suited for Python development, while Jupyter Notebook is an interactive notebook environment that is ideal for data analysis and visualization.

Regardless of which IDE you choose, you can start by
```

creating a new Python script or notebook and importing the essential libraries that you installed earlier. For example, you can import NumPy and pandas in your script using the following code:

```
```
import numpy as npimport pandas as pd
```
```

With your development environment set up, you can start writing and testing trading algorithms using the tools and libraries that you have installed. You can load historical stock price data, calculate technical indicators, backtest trading strategies, and generate buy and sell signals using the functionality provided by NumPy and pandas.

Step 4: Testing Your Trading Algorithms

Once you have written and tested your trading algorithms in Python, you can start running them in a live trading environment. There are several platforms and APIs that you can use to connect your algorithms to real-time market data and execute trades automatically.

One popular platform for algorithmic trading is MetaTrader, which is a free trading platform that supports automated trading through the use of Expert Advisors (EAs) written in MQL4 or MQL5. You can connect your Python algorithms to MetaTrader using the MetaTrader API, which allows you to send and receive data from the platform in real-time.

Another option for algorithmic trading is using a

brokerage API, such as the Interactive Brokers API or the Alpaca API, which allow you to connect your Python algorithms to your brokerage account and execute trades directly from your code. These APIs provide access to real-time market data, order execution, and portfolio management functionality, making them ideal for algorithmic traders.

Configuring Your Development Environment in python

Setting up your development environment is a crucial step in the process of writing code in Python. A well-configured environment will not only make your coding experience more efficient but also help you avoid potential errors and bugs. In this article, we will discuss the steps you need to take to configure your development environment in Python.

Install Python

The first step in configuring your development environment is to install Python. Python is a widely-used programming language that is known for its simplicity and readability. You can download the latest version of Python from the official website (https://www.python.org/) and follow the installation instructions for your operating system.

Set up a Virtual Environment

A virtual environment is a self-contained directory that contains a specific version of Python and all the packages you need for your project. Setting up a virtual environment is important because it allows you to isolate your project dependencies from other projects on your system.

To create a virtual environment, you can use the built-in venv module in Python. Open a terminal window and run the following command:

```
python3 -m venv myenv
```

This will create a new directory called myenv that contains a copy of the Python interpreter and the pip package manager. To activate the virtual environment, run the following command:

```
source myenv/bin/activate
```

You will see that your terminal prompt has changed to indicate that you are now working within the virtual environment. You can now install the packages you need for your project using pip.

Install Packages

Python has a rich ecosystem of third-party packages that you can use to extend the functionality of your code. To install a package, you can use the pip package manager. For example, to install the requests package, you can run the following command:

```
pip install requests
```

You can also create a requirements.txt file that lists all the packages you need for your project. To install the packages listed in the requirements file, run the following command:

```
pip install -r requirements.txt
```

Set up an Integrated Development Environment (IDE)

An Integrated Development Environment (IDE) is a software application that provides a comprehensive set of tools for writing, testing, and debugging code. There are many IDEs available for Python, but some popular choices include PyCharm, Visual Studio Code, and Jupyter Notebook.

Once you have chosen an IDE, you can configure it to work with your virtual environment. Most IDEs allow you to specify the Python interpreter and the virtual environment you want to use for your project. This will ensure that your code runs correctly and that you have access to all the packages you need.

Configure Code Style and Linting

Consistent code style is important for readability and maintainability. You can use tools like Pylint, Flake8, and Black to enforce code style conventions in your Python code. These tools can help you catch common errors and identify potential issues before they become a problem.

To configure code style and linting in your IDE, you can create a configuration file that specifies the rules you want to enforce. For example, you can create a .pylintrc file that contains the following settings:

```
[FORMAT]
indent-string=''
```

This will set the indent string to four spaces, which is a common convention in Python code. You can then configure your IDE to use this configuration file for linting.

Set up Version Control

Version control is essential for managing changes to your code and collaborating with other developers. Git is a popular version control system that allows you to track changes, revert to previous versions, and merge code from multiple contributors.

To set up version control for your project, you can create a Git repository and commit your code to it. You can then use commands like git add, git commit, and git push to manage your code changes.

Write Unit Tests

Unit tests are small, self-contained tests that verify the correctness of individual components of your code.

Writing unit tests is important for ensuring that your code behaves as expected and for catching bugs early in the development process.

You can use the built-in unittest module in Python to write unit tests for your code. This module provides a simple framework for defining test cases and running them automatically. You can also use third-party testing frameworks like pytest and nose to write more complex test suites.

To run your unit tests, you can use the test discovery feature in the unittest module. This feature automatically discovers test cases in your code and runs them when you run the test module.

Document Your Code

Documentation is important for making your code understandable to other developers and for providing context for future changes. You can use tools like Sphinx and Doxygen to generate documentation from your code comments.

Chapter 3: Python for Financial Applications

Python provides a wide range of libraries and tools that make it easy to analyze financial data. One of the most popular libraries for financial data analysis is pandas, which provides data structures and functions for manipulating and analyzing structured data. With pandas, you can easily load financial data from various sources, clean and preprocess the data, and perform complex data analysis tasks.

Another important library for financial data analysis in Python is NumPy, which provides support for mathematical functions and operations on arrays. NumPy is particularly useful for performing numerical calculations on financial data, such as calculating moving averages, standard deviations, and correlations.

Building Financial Models

Python is also widely used for building financial models, such as pricing models for options, bonds, and other financial instruments. One of the most popular libraries for building financial models in Python is QuantLib, which provides a wide range of functions and classes for pricing and risk management of financial instruments.

In addition to QuantLib, there are many other libraries and tools available in Python for building financial models, such as SciPy for scientific computing, SymPy for symbolic mathematics, and TensorFlow for machine learning. These libraries make it easy to implement complex financial models in Python and test them using historical data.

Automating Trading Strategies

Python is also commonly used in the financial industry for automating trading strategies. With Python, you can easily connect to various financial data sources, such as market data feeds and trading platforms, and automate the execution of trading strategies based on predefined rules and algorithms.

One of the most popular libraries for automating trading strategies in Python is backtrader, which provides a flexible and easy-to-use framework for developing and testing trading strategies. With backtrader, you can easily backtest your trading strategies using historical data, optimize the parameters of your strategies, and execute them in real-time trading environments.

In addition to backtrader, there are many other libraries and tools available in Python for automating trading strategies, such as Zipline for algorithmic trading, ccxt for connecting to cryptocurrency exchanges, and MetaTrader for forex trading. These libraries make it easy to implement and deploy automated trading strategies in Python and monitor their performance in real-time.

Conclusion

In this chapter, we have explored how Python can be used

for various financial applications, such as analyzing financial data, building financial models, and automating trading strategies. Python provides a wide range of libraries and tools that make it easy to work with financial data, implement complex financial models, and automate trading strategies.

Whether you are a financial analyst, quant developer, or algorithmic trader, Python is an essential tool for working in the financial industry. By learning Python and mastering its libraries and tools, you can gain a competitive edge in the financial industry and develop innovative solutions for analyzing financial data, building financial models, and automating trading strategies.

Advanced Python Concepts for Trading

Python is one of the most popular programming languages used in the field of trading and finance due to its simplicity, flexibility, and powerful libraries. In this article, we will explore some advanced Python concepts that are essential for trading professionals to master in order to build sophisticated trading strategies and algorithms.

Object-Oriented Programming (OOP)
Object-Oriented Programming is a programming paradigm that allows for the creation of classes and objects in Python. This concept is essential for trading professionals as it enables them to create reusable code, organize their codebase efficiently, and model real-world entities in a more intuitive way.

In Python, classes are defined using the `class` keyword, and objects are created using the `init__` method. For example, let's create a simple class called `Stock` that represents a stock trading instrument:

```python
```python class Stock:
def__init__(self, symbol, price):
self.symbol = symbol self.price = price

def update_price(self, new_price):
self.price = new_price

# Create an instance of the Stock class apple_stock =
Stock('AAPL', 150.50) print(apple_stock.symbol) #
```
```

Output: AAPLprint(apple_stock.price) # Output: 150.50

```python
# Update the price of the stock
apple_stock.update_price(155.75)
print(apple_stock.price) # Output: 155.75
```

By using OOP concepts in Python, trading professionals can create complex trading strategies, manage multiple trading instruments, and simulate trading scenarios more effectively.

Decorators
Decorators are a powerful feature in Python that allows for the modification or extension of functions or methods without changing their source code. Decorators are commonly used in trading to add additional functionality to trading algorithms, such as logging, error handling, or performance monitoring.

In Python, decorators are implemented using the `@` symbol followed by the decorator function. For example, let's create a simple decorator called `log_time` that logs the execution time of a function:

```python
import time
```

```python
def log_time(func):
def wrapper(*args, **kwargs):
start_time = time.time()
result = func(*args, **kwargs)end_time = time.time()
print(f'{func._name_} took {end_time - start_time}
seconds to execute')return result
return wrapper

@log_time
def calculate_sma(data):
# Calculate the Simple Moving Average (SMA) of a given
datasetreturn sum(data) / len(data)

# Call the calculate_sma function data = [100, 110, 120,
130, 140]
print(calculate_sma(data)) # Output: 120.0
```
```

By using decorators in Python, trading professionals can enhance the functionality of their trading algorithms, improve code readability, and reduce code duplication.

Generators
Generators are a special type of function in Python that allows for the iteration over a sequence of values without storing them in memory. Generators are particularly useful in trading for processing large datasets, streaming market data, and generating trading signals in real-time.

In Python, generators are created using the `yield` keyword inside a function. For example, let's create a simple generator called `fibonacci_sequence` that generates the Fibonacci sequence:
```

```python
def fibonacci_sequence(n):
a, b = 0, 1
for _ in range(n):
yield a
a, b = b, a + b

# Generate the first 10 numbers in the Fibonacci sequence
for num in fibonacci_sequence(10):
print(num)
```

By using generators in Python, trading professionals can optimize memory usage, improve performance, and process large datasets efficiently.

Context Managers
Context Managers are a Python feature that allows for the management of resources, such as file handles or

database connections, in a safe and efficient way. Context Managers are essential for trading professionals to ensure that resources are properly managed and released after they are no longer needed.

In Python, Context Managers are implemented using the `with` statement and the `contextlib` module. For example, let's create a simple Context Manager called `timer` that measures the execution time of a block of code:

```python
from contextlib import contextmanagerimport time

@contextmanager def timer():
start_time = time.time()yield
end_time = time.time()
print(f'The code block took {end_time - start_time} seconds to execute')

# Use the timer Context Managerwith timer():
data = [100, 110, 120, 130, 140]
sma = sum(data) / len(data)
print(f'The Simple Moving Average is {sma}')
```

Working with Python Libraries for Data Analysis

Python has become one of the most popular programming languages for data analysis due to its simplicity, versatility, and the abundance of libraries available for data manipulation and visualization. In this article, we will explore some of the most commonly used Python libraries for data analysis and discuss how they can be used effectively in various data analysis projects.

Pandas is one of the most widely used Python libraries for data analysis. It provides data structures and functions for efficiently manipulating large datasets. Pandas allows users to easily read and write data from various file formats such as CSV, Excel, and SQL databases. It also provides powerful tools for filtering, sorting, and aggregating data, making it an essential tool for cleaning and preprocessing datasets before analysis.

One of the key features of Pandas is its DataFrame object, which represents tabular data in a structured format. DataFrames can be easily manipulated using functions such as groupby, merge, and pivot_table, allowing users to perform complex data transformations with ease. Pandas also provides powerful tools for data visualization, allowing users to create plots and charts directly from their data.

Another popular Python library for data analysis is NumPy, which provides support for multidimensional arrays and mathematical functions. NumPy is particularly useful for performing numerical computations on large datasets, such as calculating means, medians, and standard deviations. NumPy also provides tools for linear algebra, Fourier transforms, and random number generation, making it a versatile library for a wide range of data analysis tasks.

Matplotlib is a powerful Python library for creating visualizations from data. It provides a wide range of plotting functions for creating line plots, bar charts, scatter plots, and more. Matplotlib allows users to customize their plots with colors, labels, and annotations, making it easy to create professional-looking visualizations for presentations and reports.

Seaborn is another popular Python library for data visualization that is built on top of Matplotlib. Seaborn provides a high-level interface for creating attractive and informative statistical plots, such as box plots, violin plots, and pair plots. Seaborn also provides tools for visualizing relationships between variables, such as scatter plots and regression plots, making it a valuable tool for exploring patterns in data.

Scikit-learn is a powerful Python library for machine learning and data analysis. It provides a wide range of algorithms for classification, regression, clustering, and dimensionality reduction. Scikit-learn also provides tools for model evaluation and selection, allowing users to compare the performance of different algorithms on their datasets.

In addition to these libraries, there are many other Python libraries available for data analysis, each with its own strengths and capabilities. Some other popular libraries include Statsmodels for statistical modeling, NetworkX for network analysis, and TensorFlow for deep learning.

When working with Python libraries for data analysis, it is important to follow best practices to ensure that your analysis is accurate and reproducible. This includes documenting your code, using version control, and testing your analysis on different datasets to ensure its robustness.

Chapter 4: Understanding Financial Markets

Financial markets play a crucial role in the global economy by facilitating the flow of funds between savers and borrowers. These markets provide a platform for individuals, businesses, and governments to raise capital, manage risk, and invest in various financial instruments. Understanding how financial markets work is essential for anyone looking to make informed decisions about their finances.

Types of Financial Markets

There are several types of financial markets, each serving a specific purpose and catering to different types of participants. The primary types of financial markets include:

Stock Market: The stock market is where shares of publicly traded companies are bought and sold. Investors can buy and sell stocks through stock exchanges like the New York Stock Exchange (NYSE) or the Nasdaq.

Bond Market: The bond market is where governments and corporations issue bonds to raise capital. Investors can buy and sell bonds through bond exchanges or over-the-counter markets.

Foreign Exchange Market: The foreign exchange market, also known as the forex market, is where currencies are traded. This market is the largest and most liquid market in the world, with trillions of dollars exchanged daily.

Commodity Market: The commodity market is where commodities like gold, oil, and agricultural products are bought and sold. Investors can trade commodities through commodity exchanges or over-the-counter markets.

Derivatives Market: The derivatives market is where financial instruments like futures, options, and swaps are traded. These instruments derive their value from underlying assets like stocks, bonds, or commodities.

Functions of Financial Markets

Financial markets serve several important functions in the economy, including:

Capital Allocation: Financial markets help allocate capital to its most productive uses by connecting savers with borrowers. Investors can invest their savings in various financial instruments, providing businesses with the capital they need to grow and expand.

Price Discovery: Financial markets facilitate price discovery by bringing buyers and sellers together to determine the fair market value of assets. Prices in financial markets are influenced by factors like supply and demand, economic conditions, and investor sentiment.

Risk Management: Financial markets allow investors to manage risk by diversifying their portfolios and hedging against potential losses. Derivatives like options and futures enable investors to protect themselves against adverse price movements.

Liquidity Provision: Financial markets provide liquidity by allowing investors to buy and sell assets quickly and easily. Liquid markets ensure that investors can access their funds when needed and reduce the risk of price manipulation.

Information Transmission: Financial markets transmit information about the economy, companies, and financial instruments through price movements and trading volumes. Investors use this information to make informed decisions about their investments.

Regulation of Financial Markets

Financial markets are regulated by government agencies and regulatory bodies to ensure transparency, fairness, and investor protection. Regulations aim to prevent fraud, market manipulation, and insider trading, as well as promote market integrity and stability.

Key regulatory bodies overseeing financial markets include the Securities and Exchange Commission (SEC) in the United States, the Financial Conduct Authority (FCA) in the United Kingdom, and the European Securities and Markets Authority (ESMA) in the European Union. These agencies enforce rules and regulations to maintain the integrity of financial markets and protect investors.

Understanding financial markets is essential for anyone

looking to navigate the complex world of finance. By learning about the different types of financial markets, their functions, and the regulations that govern them, individuals can make informed decisions about their investments and financial goals.

Financial markets play a vital role in the global economy, connecting savers with borrowers and providing a platform for capital allocation, risk management, and investment. By gaining a deeper understanding of financial markets, individuals can take control of their finances and build a secure financial future.

Financial Markets and Instruments

Financial markets are crucial components of the global economy, facilitating the exchange of assets and investments between individuals, businesses, and governments. These markets provide a platform for buying and selling financial instruments such as stocks, bonds, commodities, and derivatives. Understanding the various financial markets and instruments is essential for investors, traders, and policymakers to make informed decisions and manage risks effectively.

Financial markets can be categorized into primary and secondary markets. The primary market is where new securities are issued and sold for the first time by companies or governments to raise capital. This process is known as an initial public offering (IPO) for stocks or a bond issuance for debt securities.

The secondary market, on the other hand, is where existing securities are traded among investors without the involvement of the issuing company. The most well-known secondary market is the stock market, where shares of publicly traded companies are bought and sold on exchanges like the New York Stock Exchange (NYSE) or the Nasdaq.

Financial instruments are assets that can be traded in financial markets, representing ownership rights, debt obligations, or derivative contracts. Some common types of financial instruments include:

Stocks: Also known as equities, stocks represent ownership shares in a company. Investors who buy stocks become partial owners of the company and are entitled to a portion of its profits in the form of dividends. Stock prices fluctuate based on the company's performance, market conditions, and investor sentiment.

Bonds: Bonds are debt securities issued by governments, municipalities, or corporations to raise funds. When an investor buys a bond, they are lending money to the issuer in exchange for regular interest payments and the return of the principal amount at maturity. Bond prices are influenced by interest rates, credit ratings, and economic conditions.

Commodities: Commodities are physical goods such as gold, oil, wheat, and coffee that are traded on commodity exchanges. Investors can buy and sell commodity futures contracts, which represent agreements to buy or sell a specific quantity of a commodity at a predetermined price on a future date. Commodity prices are affected by supply and demand dynamics, geopolitical events, and weather conditions.

Derivatives: Derivatives are financial contracts that derive their value from an underlying asset, index, or interest rate. Common types of derivatives include options, futures, swaps, and forwards. Derivatives are used for hedging risks, speculating on price movements, and managing portfolio exposure. However, they can also be complex and risky instruments that require a deep understanding of market dynamics.

Financial markets play a crucial role in allocating capital efficiently and fostering economic growth. By connecting savers with borrowers, investors with companies, and buyers with sellers, financial markets enable the flow of funds to where they are needed most. Moreover, financial markets provide liquidity, price discovery, and risk management mechanisms that help investors make informed decisions and protect their investments.

Investors can access financial markets through various channels, including traditional brokerage firms, online trading platforms, and financial advisors. They can choose from a wide range of investment options based on their risk tolerance, investment goals, and time horizon. Some investors prefer to buy and hold long-term investments like stocks and bonds, while others engage in active trading of derivatives or commodities to capitalize on short-term market fluctuations.

Financial markets are influenced by a multitude of factors, including economic indicators, corporate earnings reports, geopolitical events, and central bank policies. Market participants analyze these factors to make investment decisions and anticipate market trends. For instance, a positive jobs report may boost stock prices, while a sudden interest rate hike by the Federal Reserve could lead to a sell-off in bonds.

The efficiency of financial markets depends on factors such as transparency, liquidity, and regulation. Transparency refers to the availability of information about market prices, trading volumes, and financial disclosures. Liquidity refers to the ease with which assets can be bought or sold without significantly impacting their prices. Regulation involves rules and oversight mechanisms implemented by government agencies to protect investors, ensure fair market practices, and maintain financial stability.

Financial markets are interconnected and interdependent, with developments in one market often impacting others. For example, a sharp decline in the stock market can lead to a flight to safety in the bond market, causing bond prices to rise and yields to fall. Similarly, a spike in oil prices can affect commodity markets, inflation expectations, and consumer spending patterns.

In recent years, technological advancements have transformed financial markets, making trading faster, more efficient, and accessible to a broader range of investors. Electronic trading platforms, algorithmic trading algorithms, and high-frequency trading have revolutionized the way securities are bought and sold. These technologies have increased market liquidity, reduced trading costs, and improved price discovery mechanisms.

Financial markets are not without risks, as volatility, liquidity constraints, and regulatory changes can impact investment returns. Investors should diversify their portfolios, conduct thorough research, and seek professional advice to mitigate risks and achieve their financial goals.

Key Market Concepts and Terminology

In the world of business and finance, understanding key market concepts and terminology is crucial for success. Whether you are a seasoned investor or just starting out, having a solid grasp of the language used in the markets can help you make informed decisions and navigate the complexities of the financial world. In this article, we will explore some of the most important market concepts and terminology that every investor should know.

Market Types

There are several different types of markets that investors can participate in, each with its own unique characteristics and risks. The most common types of markets include:

Stock Market: The stock market is where shares of publicly traded companies are bought and sold. Investors can buy and sell stocks through stock exchanges such as the New York Stock Exchange (NYSE) or the Nasdaq.

Bond Market: The bond market is where debt securities, or bonds, are bought and sold. Bonds are issued by governments, corporations, and other entities to raise capital. Investors can buy and sell bonds through bond exchanges or over-the-counter markets.

Commodity Market: The commodity market is where raw materials such as gold, oil, and agricultural products are bought and sold. Investors can trade commodities through commodity exchanges or through futures contracts.

Foreign Exchange Market: The foreign exchange market, also known as the forex market, is where currencies are bought and sold. Investors can trade currencies through forex brokers or through currency exchanges.

Market Participants

There are several different types of market participants who play a role in buying and selling securities. Some of the most common market participants include:

Retail Investors: Retail investors are individual investors who buy and sell securities for their personal portfolios. They typically trade through online brokerage accounts or traditional brokerage firms.

Institutional Investors: Institutional investors are large financial institutions such as mutual funds, pension funds, and hedge funds that trade on behalf of their clients. They often have access to more resources and expertise than retail investors.

Market Makers: Market makers are firms or individuals who provide liquidity to the markets by buying and selling securities. They help ensure that there is a continuous flow of trading activity and narrow bid-ask spreads.

Brokers: Brokers are intermediaries who facilitate trades between buyers and sellers. They earn a commission or fee for executing trades on behalf of their clients.

Market Orders

When placing a trade in the markets, investors can use different types of orders to specify how and when they want to buy or sell a security. Some of the most common types of market orders include:

Market Order: A market order is an order to buy or sell a security at the current market price. It is executed immediately at the best available price.

Limit Order: A limit order is an order to buy or sell a security at a specific price or better. It will only be executed if the security reaches the specified price.

Stop Order: A stop order is an order to buy or sell a security once it reaches a certain price, known as the stop price. It is used to limit losses or lock in profits.

Stop-Limit Order: A stop-limit order is a combination of a stop order and a limit order. It will trigger a limit order once the stop price is reached.

Market Indices

Market indices are used to track the performance of a specific segment of the market or the overall market. Some of the most widely followed market indices include:

S&P 500: The S&P 500 is a market index that tracks the performance of 500 of the largest publicly traded companies in the United States.

Dow Jones Industrial Average: The Dow Jones Industrial Average is a market index that tracks the performance of 30 large, publicly traded companies in the United States.

Nasdaq Composite: The Nasdaq Composite is a market index that tracks the performance of all stocks traded on the Nasdaq stock exchange.

Russell 2000: The Russell 2000 is a market index that tracks the performance of 2,000 small-cap stocks in the United States.

Market Volatility

Market volatility refers to the degree of variation in the price of a security or market index over time. High volatility indicates that prices are fluctuating rapidly, while low volatility indicates that prices are relatively stable. Volatility can be caused by a variety of factors, including economic data releases, geopolitical events, and changes in investor sentiment.

Market Capitalization

Market capitalization, or market cap, is a measure of the total value of a company's outstanding shares of stock. It is calculated by multiplying the number of outstanding shares by the current market price per share. Market capitalization is used to classify companies into different size categories, such as large-cap, mid-cap, and small-cap.

Chapter 5: Acquiring Market Data

Acquiring market data is a crucial step in any business strategy. It provides valuable insights into consumer behavior, market trends, and competitor analysis that can help guide decision-making and drive business growth. In this chapter, we will discuss the importance of acquiring market data, different sources of market data, and how to effectively utilize this information to gain a competitive advantage.

Market data is essential for businesses to understand their target market and make informed decisions. By analyzing market data, companies can identify consumer preferences, buying patterns, and trends that can help them tailor their products and services to meet customer needs. Additionally, market data can provide insights into competitor strategies, pricing, and positioning, allowing businesses to stay ahead of the competition.

There are several sources of market data that businesses can leverage to gain a comprehensive understanding of the market landscape. Primary research involves collecting data directly from consumers through surveys, focus groups, or interviews. This type of research provides firsthand insights into consumer behavior and preferences, allowing businesses to gather valuable information that may not be available through secondary sources.

Secondary research involves gathering data from existing

sources such as market reports, industry publications, and government databases. This type of research provides a broad overview of the market landscape, including industry trends, competitor analysis, and market size. By leveraging secondary research, businesses can save time and resources by accessing pre-existing data that can inform their decision-making process.

In addition to primary and secondary research, businesses can also utilize syndicated data, which is data collected by third-party providers and sold to multiple clients. Syndicated data can provide valuable insights into market trends, consumer behavior, and competitor analysis that can help businesses make informed decisions. However, it is important to carefully evaluate the quality and relevance of syndicated data to ensure its accuracy and reliability.

Once businesses have acquired market data from various sources, it is essential to effectively analyze and interpret this information to gain actionable insights. Data analysis involves identifying patterns, trends, and correlations within the data to extract meaningful insights that can inform business decisions. By utilizing data analysis tools and techniques, businesses can uncover hidden opportunities, identify potential threats, and optimize their marketing strategies to drive business growth.

In conclusion, acquiring market data is a critical step in any business strategy. By leveraging primary research, secondary research, and syndicated data, businesses can gain valuable insights into consumer behavior, market trends, and competitor analysis that can help guide decision-making and drive business growth. By effectively analyzing and interpreting market data, businesses can gain a competitive advantage and stay ahead of the competition in today's dynamic market landscape.

Sources of Historical Market Data

Historical market data is a valuable resource for investors, researchers, and analysts looking to understand the trends and patterns in financial markets over time. By analyzing historical market data, one can gain insights into the behavior of various asset classes, understand the impact of economic events on market performance, and make more informed investment decisions.

There are several sources of historical market data that can be used to conduct research and analysis. These sources vary in terms of the types of data they provide, the time periods covered, and the level of detail available. In this article, we will explore some of the most common sources of historical market data and discuss their strengths and limitations.

Stock Exchanges:

Stock exchanges are one of the primary sources of historical market data for equities. Most major stock exchanges provide historical price and volume data for individual stocks, indices, and other financial instruments traded on their platforms. This data is typically available in daily, weekly, or monthly intervals and can be accessed through the exchange's website or through data vendors that specialize in market data.

Stock exchange data is valuable for analyzing the performance of individual stocks and indices over time, identifying trends and patterns in market behavior, and conducting technical analysis. However, stock exchange data may be limited in terms of the range of financial instruments covered and the depth of historical data available.

Financial Data Providers:

Financial data providers such as Bloomberg, Thomson Reuters, and FactSet are widely used sources of historical market data for a wide range of asset classes, including equities, fixed income, commodities, and currencies.
These providers offer comprehensive databases of historical price, volume, and fundamental data that can be used for research and analysis.

Financial data providers offer a wealth of historical market data that can be accessed through their proprietary platforms or through data feeds that can be integrated into third-party software applications. These data providers also offer advanced analytics tools and research reports that can help investors make informed decisions.

Government Agencies:

Government agencies such as the U.S. Securities and Exchange Commission (SEC) and the U.S. Bureau of Economic Analysis (BEA) provide valuable historical market data on publicly traded companies, economic indicators, and other financial metrics. These agencies publish reports, filings, and datasets that can be used to analyze market trends, conduct research, and monitor regulatory developments.

Government agencies are a reliable source of historical market data that is often free or available at a low cost. However, government data may be limited in terms of the level of detail provided and the frequency of updates.

Research Firms and Academic Institutions:

Research firms and academic institutions conduct studies and publish research reports that include historical market data on various topics related to finance and economics. These reports can be valuable sources of information for investors looking to understand market trends, analyze the impact of economic events, and identify investment opportunities.

Research firms and academic institutions often publish their research findings on their websites or in academic journals, making it easy to access historical market data for a wide range of topics. However, the availability of historical data from these sources may be limited to specific research studies or time periods.

Online Databases and Archives:

There are several online databases and archives that provide access to historical market data on a wide range of asset classes and financial instruments. These databases may include historical price, volume, and fundamental data for stocks, bonds, commodities, and currencies, as well as economic indicators and macroeconomic data.

Online databases and archives are valuable sources of

historical market data that can be accessed for free or through subscription-based services. These sources often provide tools and resources for conducting research and analysis, such as data visualization tools and historical charting capabilities.

Historical market data is a valuable resource for investors, researchers, and analysts looking to understand the behavior of financial markets over time. By accessing historical market data from a variety of sources, one can gain insights into market trends, identify investment opportunities, and make more informeddecisions.

Whether you are a seasoned investor or a novice researcher, historical market data can help you navigate the complexities of the financial markets and achieve your investment goals.

Using APIs for Real-Time Data Collection python scripts

Using APIs for real-time data collection in Python scripts is a powerful way to gather and analyze data from various sources. APIs, or Application Programming Interfaces, allow different software applications to communicate with each other and exchange data. By leveraging APIs, developers can access real-time data from a wide range of sources, such as social media platforms, financial markets, weather services, and more.

In this article, we will explore how to use APIs for real-time data collection in Python scripts. We will cover the basics of working with APIs, how to authenticate and make requests to API endpoints, and how to process and analyze the data returned by the API. We will also provide examples of Python scripts that demonstrate how to collect real-time data from popular APIs.

Getting Started with APIs

Before we can start using APIs for real-time data collection in Python scripts, we need to understand the basics of working with APIs. An API is a set of rules and protocols that allows different software applications to communicate with each other. APIs define the methods and data formats that applications can use to exchange information.

To interact with an API, we typically need to make HTTP requests to specific endpoints that are provided by the API.

These endpoints represent different resources or functionalities that the API exposes. For example, a weather API might have endpoints for retrieving current weather conditions, forecasts, and historical data.

To access an API, we usually need to obtain an API key or authentication token. This key is used to authenticate our requests and ensure that we have permission to access the API. Some APIs may also require additional authentication methods, such as OAuth tokens or client certificates.

Making Requests to API Endpoints

Once we have obtained an API key or authentication token, we can start making requests to API endpoints. In Python, we can use the `requests` library to send HTTP requests to APIs and retrieve data. The `requests` library provides a simple and intuitive interface for working with APIs.

To make a request to an API endpoint, we need to specify the URL of the endpoint and any required parameters. We can use the `requests.get()` function to send a GET request to the API endpoint and retrieve the data. For example, the following code snippet demonstrates how to make a request to the OpenWeatherMap API to retrieve current weather data for a specific location:

```python
python import requests

api_key = 'YOUR_API_KEY'
url = 'http://api.openweathermap.org/data/2.5/weather'
```

```python
params = {
'q': 'New York','appid': api_key
}

response = requests.get(url, params=params) data =
response.json()

print(data)
```

In this example, we specify the API key and the URL of the
OpenWeatherMap API endpoint for retrieving current
weather data. We also provide the location (New York) as
a query parameter. The `requests.get()` function sends a
GET request to the API endpoint with the specified
parameters, and the `response.json()` method parses the
response data as a JSON object.

Processing and Analyzing API Data

Once we have retrieved data from an API endpoint, we can
process and analyze the data using Python scripts.
Depending on the structure of the data returned by the
API, we may need to extract specific information or
perform calculations on the data.

For example, if we are collecting financial data from a
stock market API, we may want to calculate the average
price of a stock over a certain time period. We can use
Python's built-in functions and libraries, such as `numpy`
and `pandas`, to perform these calculations.

```python
```

```python
import numpy as np

prices = [10.50, 11.25, 12.00, 10.75, 11.50]
average_price = np.mean(prices)

print('Average price:', average_price)
```

In this example, we calculate the average price of a stock using the `np.mean()` function from the `numpy` library. We provide a list of stock prices as input, and the function returns the average price.

Real-Time Data Collection with Python Scripts

To demonstrate how to use APIs for real-time data collection in Python scripts, let's consider a practical example of collecting real-time cryptocurrency prices from the CoinGecko API. CoinGecko is a popular cryptocurrency data platform that provides real-time market data for thousands of cryptocurrencies.

First, we need to obtain an API key from CoinGecko by signing up for an account on their website. Once we have obtained the API key, we can use it to authenticate our requests to the CoinGecko API.

```python
import requests

api_key = 'YOUR_API_KEY'

url = 'https://api.coingecko.com/api/v3/simple/price'
params = {
```

```
'ids': 'bitcoin,ethereum', 'vs_currencies': 'usd', 'api_key':
api_key
}

response = requests.get(url, params=params) data =
response.json()

bitcoin_price =
```

Chapter 6: Data Cleaning and Preprocessing

In the world of data science, one of the most important steps in the data analysis process is data cleaning and preprocessing. This chapter will delve into the various techniques and methods used to clean and preprocess data before it can be used for analysis and modeling.

Data cleaning is the process of identifying and correcting errors and inconsistencies in the data to improve its quality and accuracy. This includes handling missing values, removing duplicates, dealing with outliers, and correcting inconsistencies in the data. Data preprocessing, on the other hand, involves transforming the data into a format that is suitable for analysis and modeling. This may include scaling, normalization, encoding categorical variables, and feature engineering.

One of the first steps in data cleaning is handling missing values. Missing values can occur for a variety of reasons, such as data entry errors, equipment malfunctions, or survey non-responses. There are several techniques for handling missing values, including imputation, deletion, and prediction. Imputation involves filling in missing values with estimated values based on the rest of the data. Deletion involves removing rows or columns with missing values. Prediction involves using machine learning algorithms to predict missing values based on the rest of the data.

Another important aspect of data cleaning is removing duplicates. Duplicates can occur when the same data point is recorded multiple times, leading to inaccuracies in the analysis. Removing duplicates involves identifying and removing duplicate rows or columns from the dataset. This can be done using various techniques, such as using the drop_duplicates() function in Python or using SQL queries to identify and remove duplicates.

Dealing with outliers is another important step in data cleaning. Outliers are data points that are significantly different from the rest of the data and can skew the analysis. Outliers can be identified using statistical techniques, such as the z-score or interquartile range method. Once outliers are identified, they can be removed or transformed using techniques such as winsorization or log transformation.

Correcting inconsistencies in the data is also crucial for data cleaning. Inconsistencies can arise from data entry errors, formatting issues, or differences in data sources. This can include correcting misspellings, standardizing formats, and resolving discrepancies between different datasets. This can be done manually or using automated tools, such as regular expressions or data cleaning libraries in Python.

Data preprocessing involves transforming the data into a format that is suitable for analysis and modeling. This may include scaling the data to ensure all features are on the same scale, normalizing the data to ensure all features have the same distribution, encoding categorical variables into numerical values, and feature engineering to create new features from existing ones.

Scaling the data is important to ensure that all features are on the same scale and have equal importance in the analysis. This can be done using techniques such as min-max scaling or standardization. Normalizing the data is important to ensure that all features have the same distribution, which can improve the performance of machine learning algorithms. This can be done using techniques such as z-score normalization or log transformation.

Encoding categorical variables is important to convert categorical variables into numerical values that can be used in the analysis. This can be done using techniques such as one-hot encoding or label encoding. Feature engineering involves creating new features from existing ones to improve the performance of machine learning algorithms. This can include creating interaction terms, polynomial features, or aggregating features.

Data cleaning and preprocessing are crucial steps in the data analysis process. By identifying and correcting errors and inconsistencies in the data, and transforming the data into a format that is suitable for analysis and modeling, data scientists can ensure that their analysis is accurate and reliable.

By using the techniques and methods outlined in this chapter, data scientists can clean and preprocess their data effectively and efficiently, leading to better insights and more accurate predictions.

Techniques for Data Cleaning with python - scriptsa

Data cleaning is a crucial step in the data analysis process, as it ensures that the data is accurate, complete, and reliable. In this article, we will discuss some techniques for data cleaning using Python scripts.

Python is a popular programming language for data analysis and has a wide range of libraries and tools that can be used for data cleaning. Some of the most commonly used libraries for data cleaning in Python include Pandas, NumPy, and SciPy.

One of the most common techniques for data cleaning is handling missing values. Missing values can occur for a variety of reasons, such as data entry errors, equipment malfunctions, or simply because the data was not collected. There are several ways to handle missing values in Python, including dropping rows or columns with missing values, imputing missing values with the mean or median of the column, or using more advanced techniques such as regression or clustering.

Another important technique for data cleaning is handling outliers. Outliers are data points that are significantly different from the rest of the data and can skew the results of data analysis. There are several ways to detect and handle outliers in Python, including visualizing the data using box plots or scatter plots, calculating z-scores or interquartile ranges, or using more advanced techniques such as clustering or anomaly detection algorithms.

Data normalization is another important technique for data cleaning. Normalizing the data ensures that all the variables are on the same scale, which can improve the performance of machine learning algorithms and make the data easier to interpret. There are several ways to normalize data in Python, including scaling the data to a specific range, standardizing the data to have a mean of zero and a standard deviation of one, or using more advanced techniques such as min-max scaling or robust scaling.

Handling duplicate data is another important technique for data cleaning. Duplicate data can occur for a variety of reasons, such as data entry errors or data collection methods. There are several ways to handle duplicate data in Python, including dropping duplicate rows or columns, merging duplicate rows or columns, or using more advanced techniques such as fuzzy matching or record linkage algorithms.

Data transformation is another important technique for data cleaning. Data transformation involves converting the data into a more suitable format for analysis, such as converting categorical variables into numerical variables, encoding text data into numerical data, or transforming skewed data distributions into more normal distributions. There are several ways to transform data in Python, including using one-hot encoding, label encoding, or log transformations.

In this section, we will provide an example of data cleaning using Python scripts. We will use the Pandas library, which is a powerful library for data manipulation and analysis in Python.

First, we will import the necessary libraries:

```python
import pandas as pdimport numpy as np
```

Next, we will create a sample dataset with missing values, outliers, and duplicate data:

```python
data = {
'A': [1, 2, np.nan, 4, 5],
'B': [10, 20, 30, 40, 50],
'C': [100, 200, 300, 400, 500],
'D': [1, 2, 3, 4, 5]
}

df = pd.DataFrame(data)
df = df.append(df) # duplicate data df.iloc[0, 0] = 1000 #
outlier
```

Now, let's handle missing values by dropping rows with missing values:

```python
df.dropna(inplace=True)
```

Next, let's handle outliers by removing rows with outliers:

```python
```

```python
df = df[(np.abs(df-df.mean()) <= (3*df.std())).all(axis=1)]
```

Now, let's handle duplicate data by dropping duplicate rows:

```python
df.drop_duplicates(inplace=True)
```

Finally, let's transform the data by standardizing the data:

```python
df = (df - df.mean()) / df.std()
```

By following these techniques for data cleaning, we have successfully cleaned the sample dataset using Python scripts. Data cleaning is an essential step in the data analysis process, as it ensures that the data is accurate, complete, and reliable. Python is a powerful tool for data cleaning, with a wide range of libraries and tools that can be used to handle missing values, outliers, duplicate data, and transform the data into a more suitable format for analysis. By using Python scripts for data cleaning, analysts can ensure that their data is clean and ready for further analysis and interpretation.

Handling Missing and Outlier Data with python

Data preprocessing is an essential step in any data analysis or machine learning project. One of the common challenges in data preprocessing is handling missing and outlier data. Missing data can arise due to various reasons such as data collection errors, data entry mistakes, or simply because the data is not available. Outliers, on the other hand, are data points that deviate significantly from the rest of the data and can skew the analysis results.

In this article, we will discuss how to handle missing and outlier data using Python, a popular programming language for data analysis and machine learning.

Handling Missing Data:

Missing data can have a significant impact on the analysis results and can lead to biased or inaccurate conclusions. There are several ways to handle missing data in Python, including:

Dropping missing values:
One of the simplest ways to handle missing data is to simply drop the rows or columns that contain missing values. This can be done using the dropna() function in pandas, a popular data manipulation library in Python.

```python
import pandas as pd

# Create a DataFrame with missing values data = {'A': [1, 2,
```

```
None, 4],
'B': [5, None, 7, 8]}
df = pd.DataFrame(data)

# Drop rows with missing valuesdf.dropna()
```

Imputing missing values:
Another approach to handling missing data is to impute the missing values with a suitable value. This can be done using the fillna() function in pandas.

```python
# Impute missing values with the meandf.fillna(df.mean())
```

Using machine learning algorithms:
Another approach to handling missing data is to use machine learning algorithms to predict the missing values. This can be done using algorithms such as K-Nearest Neighbors or Decision Trees.

```python
from sklearn.impute import KNNImputer

# Create a KNN imputer imputer = KNNImputer()

# Impute missing values
imputed_data = imputer.fit_transform(df)
```

Handling Outlier Data:

Outliers can significantly affect the analysis results and can lead to inaccurate conclusions. There are several ways to handle outlier data in Python, including:

Identifying outliers:
The first step in handling outlier data is to identify the outliers in the dataset. This can be done using statistical methods such as Z-Score or IQR (Interquartile Range).

```python
import numpy as np

# Calculate Z-Score
z_scores = np.abs((df - df.mean()) / df.std())

# Identify outliers
outliers = df[z_scores > 3]
```

Removing outliers:
One approach to handling outlier data is to simply remove the outliers from the dataset. This can be done by filtering

the data based on the identified outliers.

```python
# Remove outliers
filtered_data = df[(z_scores < 3).all(axis=1)]
```

Transforming outliers:
Another approach to handling outlier data is to transform the outliers to bring them closer to the rest of the data. This can be done using techniques such as winsorization or log transformation.

```python
# Winsorize outliers
from scipy.stats.mstats import winsorize winsorized_data = winsorize(df, limits=[0.05, 0.05])
```

We discussed how to handle missing and outlier data using Python. Missing data can be handled by dropping missing values, imputing missing values, or using machine learning algorithms. Outlier data can be handled by identifying outliers, removing outliers, or transforming outliers. It is important to carefully consider the best approach for handling missing and outlier data based on the specific characteristics of the dataset and the analysis objectives.

Python provides a wide range of tools and libraries for handling missing and outlier data, making it a powerful platform for data preprocessing in data analysis and machine learning projects.

Chapter 7: Exploratory Data Analysis (EDA)

Exploratory Data Analysis, commonly referred to as EDA, is a critical step in the data analysis process. It involves the initial investigation of data to discover patterns, identify anomalies, and test hypotheses before applying more advanced statistical techniques. EDA is an essential tool for data scientists, statisticians, and researchers to gain a better understanding of the data they are working with and to make informed decisions about how to proceed with their analysis.

In this chapter, we will explore the key concepts and techniques involved in EDA, including data visualization, summary statistics, and data cleaning. We will also discuss the importance of EDA in the data analysis process and provide examples of how it can be used to uncover insights and drive decision-making.

Data Visualization

Data visualization is a powerful tool in EDA that allows us to explore patterns and relationships in the data. By representing data graphically, we can quickly identify trends, outliers, and other important features that may not be apparent from looking at the raw data. Common types of data visualizations include scatter plots, histograms, box plots, and bar charts.

Scatter plots are used to visualize the relationship between two variables. By plotting one variable on the x-axis and another on the y-axis, we can see if there is a correlation or pattern between the two variables. Histograms are used to display the distribution of a single variable, showing the frequency of different values within a dataset. Box plots are useful for visualizing the spread of data and identifying outliers, while bar charts are commonly used to compare the frequency of different categories within a dataset.

Summary Statistics

Summary statistics are another important component of EDA that provide a concise summary of the main characteristics of a dataset. Common summary statistics include measures of central tendency (such as mean, median, and mode), measures of dispersion (such as standard deviation and range), and measures of skewness and kurtosis.

Central tendency measures provide information about the average value of a dataset, while measures of dispersion give us an idea of how spread out the data is. Skewness and kurtosis measures provide information about the shape of the distribution of the data, helping us to understand if the data is symmetric or skewed.

Data Cleaning

Data cleaning is an essential step in EDA that involves identifying and correcting errors, inconsistencies, and missing values in a dataset. Cleaning the data ensures that our analysis is based on accurate and reliable information, leading to more robust and trustworthy results.

Common data cleaning tasks include removing duplicates, handling missing values, correcting data entry errors, and standardizing data formats. By cleaning the data before conducting further analysis, we can avoid bias and ensure that our conclusions are based on high-quality data.

Importance of EDA

EDA plays a crucial role in the data analysis process by helping us to understand the data, identify patterns and relationships, and generate insights that can drive decision-making. By conducting EDA before applying more complex statistical techniques, we can gain a deeper understanding of the data and make more informed choicesabout how to proceed with our analysis.

EDA allows us to explore the data visually, identify outliers and anomalies, and test hypotheses before conducting formal statistical tests. It also helps us to identify potential data quality issues and make decisions about how to clean and preprocess the data before conducting further analysis.

Exploratory Data Analysis is a critical step in the data analysis process that helps us to gain a better understanding of the data we are working with and make informed decisions about how to proceed with our analysis. By using data visualization, summary statistics, and data cleaning techniques, we can uncover patterns, relationships, and insights that can drive decision-making and lead to more robust and reliable results.

Statistical Analysis of Financial Data with python

Statistical analysis of financial data is a crucial aspect of financial decision-making. By analyzing historical data, trends, and patterns, analysts can make informed decisions about investments, risk management, and portfolio optimization. Python is a popular programming language for statistical analysis due to its powerful libraries and tools for data manipulation, visualization, and modeling. In this article, we will explore how to perform statistical analysis of financial data using Python.

Importing Data

The first step in conducting statistical analysis of financial data is to import the data into Python. There are several ways to import financial data, such as using APIs to connect to financial databases or downloading data from financial websites. One of the most common ways to import financial data is to use the pandas library in Python, which provides a convenient way to work with structured data.

import pandas as pd
data = pd.read_csv('financial_data.csv') Descriptive Statistics
Descriptive statistics are used to summarize and describe the main features of a dataset. This includes measures of central tendency, dispersion, and shape of the data. Some common descriptive statistics include mean, median, standard deviation, and skewness. Let's calculate some descriptive statistics for our financial data.

```python
mean = data['price'].mean()   median = data['price'].median()   std_dev = data['price'].std()
skewness = data['price'].skew()

print('Mean:', mean)   print('Median:', median)
print('Standard Deviation:', std_dev)   print('Skewness:', skewness)
```

Correlation Analysis

Correlation analysis is used to measure the strength and direction of the relationship between two variables. In financial analysis, correlation analysis is often used to understand the relationship between different financial instruments or asset classes. We can calculate the correlation matrix for our financial data using the corr() function in pandas.

```python
correlation_matrix = data.corr()print(correlation_matrix)
```

Visualization

Visualization is an essential part of statistical analysis as it helps in understanding the data and identifying patterns and trends. Python provides powerful libraries such as matplotlib and seaborn for creating visualizations. Let's create a line plot to visualize the trend of stock prices over time.

```python
import matplotlib.pyplot as plt plt.plot(data['date'], data['price'])plt.xlabel('Date') plt.ylabel('Price') plt.title('Stock Price Trend')plt.show()
```

Hypothesis Testing

Hypothesis testing is used to make inferences about a population based on sample data. In financial analysis, hypothesis testing can be used to test the significance of relationships or differences between variables. We can perform hypothesis testing using the scipy library in Python. Let's perform a t-test to compare the mean stock prices of two different companies.

```python
from scipy.stats import ttest_ind
company1_prices = data[data['company'] == 'Company1']['price'] company2_prices = data[data['company'] == 'Company2']['price']

t_stat, p_value = ttest_ind(company1_prices, company2_prices)print('T-statistic:', t_stat) print('P-value:', p_value)
```

Time Series Analysis
Time series analysis is used to analyze and forecast time-series data, such as stock prices, interest rates, and economic indicators. Python provides the statsmodels library for time series analysis, which includes functions for modeling and forecasting time series data. Let's fit an ARIMA model to our financial data and make a forecast.

```
from statsmodels.tsa.arima.model import ARIMAmodel =
ARIMA(data['price'],   order=(1,   1,   1))   model_fit   =
model.fit()
forecast  =  model_fit.forecast(steps=10)  print('Forecast:',
forecast)
```

We have explored how to perform statistical analysis of financial data using Python. We have covered importing data, calculating descriptive statistics, correlation analysis, visualization, hypothesis testing, and time series analysis.

Python provides a powerful and flexible environment for conducting statistical analysis, making it a valuable tool for financial analysts and researchers. By leveraging Python's libraries and tools, analysts can gain valuable insights from financial data and make informed decisions about investments and riskmanagement.

Visualization Techniques for Market Trends with Python - scripts

In today's fast-paced business world, staying ahead of market trends is crucial for success. One way to gain insights into market trends is through data visualization techniques. By using Python scripts, analysts can create visually appealing and informative charts and graphs that help to identify patterns and make informed decisions.

Python is a popular programming language that is widely used for data analysis and visualization. It offers a variety of libraries and tools that make it easy to create stunning visualizations from raw data. In this article, we will explore some visualization techniques for market trends using Python scripts.

Line Charts

One of the most common ways to visualize market trends is through line charts. Line charts are effective for showing trends over time, making them ideal for tracking stock prices, sales figures, and other time-series data. In Python, you can create a line chart using the Matplotlib library, which provides a simple and intuitive interface for plotting data.

Here's an example of how to create a basic line chart in Python:

```python
import matplotlib.pyplot as plt
```

```
# Data
x = [1, 2, 3, 4, 5]
y = [10, 20, 15, 25, 30]

# Create a line chart plt.plot(x, y) plt.xlabel('Time')
plt.ylabel('Value') plt.title('Market Trends')plt.show()
```

In this example, we create a line chart with the x-axis representing time and the y-axis representing the value of a particular market trend. By plotting this data, we can easily see how the trend has evolved over time.

Bar Charts

Another useful visualization technique for market trends is the bar chart. Bar charts are ideal for comparing different categories or groups of data, making them useful for visualizing market share, sales by region, and other categorical data. In Python, you can create a bar chart using the Matplotlib library as well.

Here's an example of how to create a basic bar chart in Python:

```python
import matplotlib.pyplot as plt
```

```
# Data
categories = ['A', 'B', 'C', 'D']values = [10, 20, 15, 25]

# Create a bar chart plt.bar(categories, values)
plt.xlabel('Category') plt.ylabel('Value')
plt.title('Market Trends by Category')plt.show()
```

In this example, we create a bar chart with the x-axis representing different categories and the y-axis representing the values of each category. By plotting this data, we can easily compare the market trends across different categories.

Scatter Plots

Scatter plots are another powerful visualization technique for market trends. Scatter plots are useful for showing the relationship between two variables, making them ideal for identifying correlations and patterns in the data. In Python, you can create a scatter plot using the Matplotlib library.

Here's an example of how to create a basic scatter plot in Python:

```python
import matplotlib.pyplot as plt

# Data
x = [1, 2, 3, 4, 5]
y = [10, 20, 15, 25, 30]
```

```
# Create a scatter plot plt.scatter(x, y) plt.xlabel('Variable
1')
plt.ylabel('Variable      2')      plt.title('Market      Trends
Relationship')plt.show()
```

In this example, we create a scatter plot with the x-axis representing one variable and the y-axis representing another variable. By plotting this data, we can easily see if there is a relationship between the two variables.

Pie Charts

Pie charts are a simple yet effective visualization technique for market trends. Pie charts are ideal for showing the distribution of a single variable, making them useful for visualizing market share, sales by product, and other

categorical data. In Python, you can create a pie chart using the Matplotlib library. Here's an example of how to create a basic pie chart in Python:

```python
import matplotlib.pyplot as plt

# Data
labels = ['A', 'B', 'C', 'D']sizes = [25, 35, 20, 20]

# Create a pie chart
plt.pie(sizes,       labels=labels,       autopct='%1.1f%%')
plt.title('Market Trends Distribution')
plt.show()
```

```
```

We create a pie chart showing the distribution of market trends across different categories. By plotting this data, we can easily see the relative proportions of each category.

Visualization techniques are powerful tools for analyzing market trends and making informed decisions. By using Python scripts and libraries like Matplotlib, analysts can create a wide variety of charts and graphs that help to identify patterns, correlations, and trends in the data.

Whether you're tracking stock prices, sales figures, or market share, Python offers a flexible and intuitive platform for visualizing market trends. By incorporating these visualization techniques into your analysis workflow, you can gain valuable insights into

Chapter 8: Introduction to Trading Strategies

In the world of finance and investing, trading strategies are essential tools that help traders make informed decisions about buying and selling assets in financial markets. These strategies are designed to maximize profits and minimize risks by taking advantage of market trends and patterns. In this chapter, we will explore the various types of trading strategies, their benefits, and how they can be implemented effectively.

Types of Trading Strategies

There are several types of trading strategies that traders can use to achieve their financial goals. Some of the most common trading strategies include:

Trend following: This strategy involves identifying and following the direction of market trends. Traders who use this strategy aim to buy assets that are trending upwards and sell assets that are trending downwards. Trend following strategies are based on the belief that trends tend to continue in the same direction for a period of time.

Range trading: Range trading involves buying assets at the lower end of a price range and selling them at the upper end of the range. This strategy is based on the belief that assets tend to trade within a certain price range over a period of time.

Momentum trading: Momentum trading involves buying assets that are gaining momentum and selling assets that are losing momentum. This strategy is based on the belief that assets that are gaining momentum are likely to continue to rise in price, while assets that are losing momentum are likely to continue to fall in price.

Mean reversion: Mean reversion trading involves buying assets that are undervalued and selling assets that are overvalued. This strategy is based on the belief that assets tend to revert to their mean value over time.

Benefits of Trading Strategies

Trading strategies offer several benefits to traders, including:

Increased profitability: Trading strategies help traders make informed decisions about when to buy and sell assets, which can lead to increased profitability. By following a trading strategy, traders can take advantage of market trends and patterns to maximize their profits.

Risk management: Trading strategies help traders minimize risks by providing guidelines for when to enter and exit trades. By following a trading strategy, traders can reduce the likelihood of making impulsive decisions that could result in losses.

Consistency: Trading strategies help traders maintain consistency in their trading approach. By following a set of rules and guidelines, traders can avoid emotional decision-making and stick to a disciplined trading plan.

Adaptability: Trading strategies can be adapted to different market conditions and asset classes. Traders can customize their trading strategies to suit their individual trading styles and preferences.

Implementing Trading Strategies

To implement a trading strategy effectively, traders should follow these key steps:

Define the trading strategy: Traders should clearly define the objectives, rules, and guidelines of the trading strategy. This includes identifying the assets to trade, the entry and exit points, and the risk management rules.

Backtest the strategy: Traders should backtest the trading strategy using historical data to evaluate its performance. Backtesting helps traders identify any weaknesses or flaws in the strategy and make necessary adjustments.

Paper trade the strategy: Traders should paper trade the trading strategy in a simulated trading environment before risking real capital. Paper trading allows traders to practice implementing the strategy and gain confidence in its effectiveness.

Monitor and evaluate the strategy: Traders should continuously monitor and evaluate the performance of the trading strategy. This includes tracking the profitability, risk-adjusted returns, and other key metrics to assess the effectiveness of the strategy.

Trading strategies are essential tools that help traders make informed decisions about buying and selling assets in financial markets. By understanding the different types of trading strategies, their benefits, and how to implement them effectively, traders can improve their trading performance and achieve their financial goals.

Whether you are a novice trader or an experienced investor, trading strategies can help you navigate the complexities of financial markets and make profitable trades.

Types of Trading Strategies: Trend Following, Mean Reversion, Arbitrage

Trading strategies are essential tools for investors and traders to maximize profits and minimize risks in the financial markets. There are various types of trading strategies that traders can use to achieve their investment goals. In this article, we will discuss three popular trading strategies: trend following, mean reversion, and arbitrage.

Trend Following

Trend following is a trading strategy that involves identifying and following the direction of a market trend. Traders who use this strategy believe that markets tend to move in trends, and by following these trends, they can profit from the momentum of the market. Trend following is based on the principle that the trend is your friend, and traders should ride the trend until it shows signs of reversal.

There are several ways to identify trends in the market, including using technical analysis tools such as moving averages, trend lines, and momentum indicators. Traders can also use fundamental analysis to identify trends based on economic data, company earnings, and other factors that can influence the market.

Once a trend is identified, traders can enter a trade in the direction of the trend and hold onto it until the trend shows signs of weakening or reversing. Trend following traders typically use stop-loss orders to protect their profits and limit their losses.

Mean Reversion

Mean reversion is a trading strategy that involves identifying markets that are overbought or oversold and betting on a reversal to the mean. Traders who use this strategy believe that markets tend to revert to their average or mean price over time, and they can profit from these mean-reverting movements.

To identify mean-reverting opportunities, traders can use technical indicators such as RSI (Relative Strength Index), Bollinger Bands, and MACD (Moving Average Convergence Divergence). These indicators can help traders identify when a market is overbought or oversold and ripe for a mean-reverting trade.

Mean reversion traders typically enter a trade when a market is at an extreme level and bet on a reversal to the mean. They can also use stop-loss orders to protect their profits and limit their losses.

Arbitrage

Arbitrage is a trading strategy that involves exploiting price differences in the same asset or related assets in different markets. Traders who use this strategy look for opportunities to buy an asset at a lower price in one market and sell it at a higher price in another market, profiting from the price difference.

There are several types of arbitrage strategies, including:

Spatial arbitrage: This involves exploiting price differences in the same asset in different geographic locations. For example, a trader may buy a stock in one market where it is trading at a lower price and sell it in another market where it is trading at a higher price.

Temporal arbitrage: This involves exploiting price differences in the same asset at different points in time. For example, a trader may buy a futures contract for an asset at a lower price and sell it at a higher price when the contract expires.

Statistical arbitrage: This involves exploiting price differences in related assets based on statistical models. For example, a trader may buy one stock and sell another stock that is highly correlated with it, profiting from the price difference between the two assets.

Arbitrage traders typically use automated trading systems and algorithms to identify and execute arbitrage opportunities quickly and efficiently. They also need to have access to multiple markets and trading platforms to take advantage of arbitrage opportunities.

Trading strategies are essential tools for investors and traders to achieve their investment goals in the financial markets. Trend following, mean reversion, and arbitrage are three popular trading strategies that traders can use to maximize profits and minimize risks. By understanding these strategies and how they work, traders can make informed decisions and improve their trading performance.

Backtesting Strategies: Concepts and Best Practices

Backtesting strategies is a crucial aspect of trading and investing in the financial markets. It involves testing a trading strategy using historical data to see how it would have performed in the past. This allows traders and investors to evaluate the effectiveness of their strategies and make necessary adjustments before risking real money in the markets.

Concepts of Backtesting Strategies

There are several key concepts that traders and investors need to understand when it comes to backtesting strategies. These include:

Historical Data: Backtesting requires historical data to simulate trades and evaluate the performance of a trading strategy. This data typically includes price, volume, and other relevant information for the financial instrument being traded.

Trading Strategy: A trading strategy is a set of rules and criteria that determine when to enter and exit trades. It is essential to have a clear and well-defined strategy before backtesting to ensure accurate results.

Backtesting Software: There are many backtesting software programs available that allow traders to test their strategies using historical data. These programs often provide tools for analyzing results and optimizing strategies.

Optimization: Optimization involves adjusting the parameters of a trading strategy to improve its performance. This can be done through backtesting to identify the most profitable settings for the strategy.

Risk Management: Backtesting should also consider risk management principles to ensure that the strategy is not overly risky. This includes setting stop-loss levels and position sizing based on the strategy's historical performance.

Best Practices for Backtesting Strategies

To get the most out of backtesting, traders and investors should follow these best practices:

Use Quality Data: It is essential to use high-quality historical data for backtesting to ensure accurate results. This data should be clean, accurate, and free from errors or inconsistencies.

Define Clear Goals: Before backtesting a strategy, traders should define clear goals and objectives. This includes determining the desired level of profitability, risk tolerance, and other key metrics.

Test Multiple Timeframes: It is important to test a trading strategy across multiple timeframes to ensure its effectiveness in different market conditions. This can help identify any weaknesses or limitations in the strategy.

Include Transaction Costs: Backtesting should account for transaction costs, such as commissions and slippage, to provide a more realistic assessment of a strategy's performance.

Monitor Results: Traders should regularly monitor the results of their backtesting to identify any issues or areas for improvement. This can help refine the strategy and make necessary adjustments.

Avoid Overfitting: Overfitting occurs when a trading strategy is optimized too much for historical data, leading to poor performance in real-time trading. Traders should be cautious of overfitting and focus on robust strategies that perform well across different market conditions.

Backtest Regularly: Backtesting should be an ongoing process to ensure that a trading strategy remains effective over time. Traders should regularly backtest their strategies and make adjustments as needed.

Backtesting strategies is a crucial step in trading and investing that can help improve performance and profitability. By understanding key concepts and following best practices, traders can effectively test their strategies and make informed decisions in the financial markets.

Chapter 9: Trend Following Strategies

Trend following strategies are a popular approach to trading in the financial markets. This chapter will explore the concept of trend following, why it is used by traders, and how to implement trend following strategies effectively.

What is Trend Following?

Trend following is a trading strategy that involves identifying and following the direction of a market trend. Traders who use trend following strategies believe that prices tend to move in a particular direction for an extended period of time, and that by following these trends, they can profit from the market's momentum.

Trend following strategies can be applied to various financial markets, including stocks, commodities, and currencies. Traders can use technical analysis tools such as moving averages, trend lines, and momentum indicators to identify trends and make trading decisions based on them.

Why Use Trend Following Strategies?

There are several reasons why traders use trend following strategies. One of the main reasons is that trends tend to persist over time, allowing traders to ride the momentum of the market and potentially profit from large price movements.

Another reason is that trend following strategies can help traders to avoid emotional decision-making. By following a predefined set of rules based on market trends, traders can reduce the impact of fear and greed on their trading decisions and stick to a disciplined approach.

Additionally, trend following strategies can be used in both bullish and bearish markets, making them a versatile tool for traders in any market environment.

Implementing Trend Following Strategies

There are several key steps to implementing trend following strategies effectively. The first step is to identify the trend in the market using technical analysis tools. This may involve looking at price charts, moving averages, and other indicators to determine the direction of the trend.

Once the trend has been identified, traders can then enter trades in the direction of the trend. This may involve buying securities that are in an uptrend or selling securities that are in a downtrend. Traders can use stop-loss orders to manage risk and protect their capital in case the trend reverses.

It is important for traders to have a clear set of rules for entering and exiting trades based on market trends. This may involve setting specific price targets, using trailing stop-loss orders, or using other risk management techniques to maximize profits and minimize losses.

Moving Averages and Momentum Indicators Trading

Moving averages and momentum indicators are two popular tools used by traders to analyze price trends and make informed trading decisions. These indicators help traders identify potential entry and exit points in the market, as well as gauge the strength and direction of a trend. In this article, we will explore the basics of moving averages and momentum indicators trading, and how they can be used effectively in your trading strategy.

Moving averages are a technical analysis tool that smooths out price data by creating a constantly updated average price. There are different types of moving averages, including simple moving averages (SMA), exponential moving averages (EMA), and weighted moving averages (WMA). The most commonly used moving averages are the 50-day and 200-day moving averages, which are used to identify short-term and long-term trends in the market.

One of the main uses of moving averages is to identify trends in the market. When the price is above the moving average, it is considered a bullish trend, and when the price is below the moving average, it is considered a bearish trend. Traders use moving averages to confirm the direction of a trend and to filter out noise in the market. By using multiple moving averages with different time periods, traders can identify potential entry and exit points in the market.

Another popular technical indicator used by traders is

momentum indicators. Momentum indicators measure the rate of change in price movements and help traders identify overbought or oversold conditions in the market. Some of the most commonly used momentum indicators include the Relative Strength Index (RSI), the Stochastic Oscillator, and the Moving Average Convergence Divergence (MACD).

Momentum indicators are used to confirm the strength of a trend and to identify potential reversal points in the market. When a momentum indicator reaches extreme levels, it can signal that the market is overbought or oversold, and a reversal may be imminent. Traders use momentum indicators in conjunction with other technical analysis tools to make informed trading decisions and to maximize their profits.

When it comes to trading with moving averages and momentum indicators, there are several strategies that traders can use to maximize their profits. One popular strategy is the moving average crossover strategy, where traders buy when the short-term moving average crosses above the long-term moving average, and sell when the short-term moving average crosses below the long-term moving average. This strategy helps traders identify potential trend reversals in the market and capitalize on them.

Another popular strategy is the momentum divergence strategy, where traders look for divergences between price and momentum indicators to identify potential reversal points in the market. When the price is making higher highs, but the momentum indicator is making lower highs, it can signal that the trend is losing momentum and a reversal may be imminent. Traders use this strategy to enter and exit trades at the most opportune times and to maximize their profits.

Moving averages and momentum indicators are powerful tools that can help traders analyze price trends and make informed trading decisions. By using these indicators in conjunction with other technical analysis tools, traders can identify potential entry and exit points in the market, confirm the strength of a trend, and maximize their profits.

Whether you are a beginner or an experienced trader, incorporating moving averages and momentum indicators into your trading strategy can help you become a more successful and profitable trader.

Implementing Trend Following Algorithms in Python - scripts

Trend following is a popular trading strategy that involves analyzing the direction of an asset's price movement over time and making decisions based on the trend. In this article, we will discuss how to implement trend following algorithms in Python using scripts examples.

Python is a versatile programming language that is widely used in the financial industry for algorithmic trading. It provides a rich set of libraries and tools that make it easy to implement complex trading strategies.

To implement trend following algorithms in Python, we will use the pandas library for data manipulation and the matplotlib library for data visualization. We will also use the numpy library for numerical computations.

To begin, let's first define what a trend following algorithm is. A trend following algorithm is a trading strategy that aims to capture gains by following an established trend in the market. This strategy involves buying an asset when its price is rising and selling it when its price is falling.

One of the most popular trend following indicators is the moving average. A moving average is a simple technical analysis tool that smooths out price data by creating a constantly updated average price. By comparing the current price to the moving average, traders can identify trends and make trading decisions.

Let's start by implementing a simple trend following algorithm in Python using the moving average indicator. We will use historical price data for a stock and calculate its moving average over a certain period of time.

```python
import pandas as pdimport numpy as np
import matplotlib.pyplot as plt

# Load historical price data
data = pd.read_csv('stock_data.csv')

# Calculate moving average
data['MA'] = data['Close'].rolling(window=20).mean()

# Plot price data and moving average
plt.figure(figsize=(12,6))                plt.plot(data['Close'],
label='Price') plt.plot(data['MA'], label='Moving Average')
plt.legend()
plt.show()
```

In this script, we first load historical price data for a stock from a CSV file. We then calculate the 20-day moving average of the stock's closing price and plot both the price data and the moving average on a line chart.

Next, let's implement a simple trend following strategy based on the moving average indicator. In this strategy, we will buy the stock when its price crosses above the moving average and sell it when its price crosses below the moving average.

```python
# Initialize trading signalsdata['Signal'] = 0

# Generate trading signals
data['Signal'][20:]    =    np.where(data['Close'][20:]    >
data['MA'][20:], 1, 0)data['Position'] = data['Signal'].diff()

#    Plot    trading    signals    plt.figure(figsize=(12,6))
plt.plot(data['Close'],    label='Price')    plt.plot(data['MA'],
label='Moving Average')
plt.plot(data[data['Position']         ==         1].index,
data['MA'][data['Position']  ==  1],  '^',  markersize=10,
color='g', lw=0,label='Buy Signal')
plt.plot(data[data['Position']         ==         -1].index,
data['MA'][data['Position']  ==  -1],  'v',  markersize=10,
color='r', lw=0,label='Sell Signal')
plt.legend() plt.show()
```

In this script, we first initialize a column in the data frame
to store trading signals. We then generate buy signalswhen
the stock's price crosses above the moving average and sell
signals when the price crosses below the moving average.
Finally, we plot the trading signals on the price chart.

Implementing trend following algorithms in Python can be
a powerful tool for traders looking to capitalize on market
trends. By using simple technical indicators like moving
averages, traders can identify trends and make informed
trading decisions.

In addition to moving averages, there are many other
trend following indicators that traders can use, such as the

Relative Strength Index (RSI), the Moving Average Convergence Divergence (MACD), and the Average Directional Index (ADX). These indicators can help traders identify trends, confirm trend strength, and determine when a trend is reversing.

When implementing trend following algorithms in Python, it is important to backtest the strategy using historical data to evaluate its performance. By backtesting the strategy, traders can assess its profitability, risk, and overall effectiveness before deploying it in live trading.

Implementing trend following algorithms in Python can be a valuable tool for traders looking to capitalize on market trends. By using simple technical indicators and backtesting strategies, traders can make informed trading decisions and improve their overall trading performance.

Chapter 10: Mean Reversion Strategies trading

Mean reversion strategies are a popular trading approach that involves identifying assets that have deviated from their historical average prices and betting on them to revert back to the mean. In this chapter, we will delve into the details of mean reversion strategies trading, including the key concepts, techniques, and best practices for successful implementation.

Mean reversion is based on the idea that prices tend to fluctuate around a long-term average over time. When prices deviate significantly from this average, there is a tendency for them to revert back to it. This presents an opportunity for traders to profit by betting on the reversal of these price movements.

One of the key concepts in mean reversion trading is the use of statistical measures to identify assets that are overvalued or undervalued. Common indicators used in mean reversion strategies include the moving average, Bollinger Bands, and the Relative Strength Index (RSI). These indicators help traders identify assets that have strayed too far from their average prices and are likely to revert back in the near future.

Another important aspect of mean reversion strategies trading is risk management. Since mean reversion trading involves betting on assets to revert back to their mean prices, there is a risk of the trade not working out as expected. To mitigate this risk, traders should use stop-loss orders to limit potential losses and set realistic profit targets to lock in gains.

In addition to risk management, successful mean reversion trading also requires a disciplined approach to decision-making. Traders should stick to their trading plan and avoid emotional decision-making based on short-term market fluctuations. By following a systematic approach to trading, traders can increase their chances of success in mean reversion strategies.

One of the key techniques used in mean reversion trading is pairs trading. Pairs trading involves identifying two assets that are closely related and trading them simultaneously based on their relative price movements. By betting on the convergence of the prices of these two assets, traders can profit from mean reversion in a market-neutral manner.

Another technique used in mean reversion trading is mean reversion backtesting. Backtesting involves testing a trading strategy on historical data to evaluate its performance and identify potential weaknesses. By backtesting mean reversion strategies on historical data, traders can refine their approach and increase their chances of success in live trading.

Mean reversion strategies trading is a popular approach that involves identifying assets that have deviated from their historical average prices and betting on them to revert back to the mean. By using statistical measures, risk management techniques, and disciplined decision-making, traders can increase their chances of success in mean reversion trading. Pairs trading and mean reversion backtesting are key techniques that can help traders refine their approach and improve their trading performance. Overall, mean reversion strategies trading offers a systematic and disciplined approach to profiting from market inefficiencies and price movements.

The Theory of Mean Reversion in trading

Mean reversion is a trading strategy that is based on the idea that asset prices tend to revert to their historical averages over time. This theory suggests that when an asset's price deviates significantly from its average price, it is likely to move back towards that average in the future. Traders who follow the mean reversion strategy aim to profit from these price movements by buying assets that are trading below their historical averages and selling assets that are trading above their historical averages.

The theory of mean reversion is based on the belief that markets are inefficient and that prices do not always reflect the true value of an asset. This inefficiency can create opportunities for traders to profit from short-term price movements that are not justified by the underlying fundamentals of the asset. By identifying assets that are trading at extreme levels relative to their historical averages, traders can take advantage of these temporary price discrepancies and generate profits as prices revert back to their mean.

There are several key principles that underlie the theory of mean reversion. The first principle is that asset prices tend to fluctuate around their long-term average value. This means that when an asset's price deviates significantly from its average price, it is likely to move back towards that average in the future. This tendency for prices to revert to their mean is known as mean reversion.

The second principle of mean reversion is that extreme

price movements are often followed by a period of consolidation or reversal. When an asset's price moves significantly above or below its historical average, it is likely to experience a period of consolidation as the market adjusts to the new price level. This consolidation phase is often followed by a reversal in the price trend as the asset moves back towards its mean.

The third principle of mean reversion is that price movements are driven by a combination of fundamental factors and market psychology. While fundamental factors such as earnings, economic data, and company news can influence asset prices in the short term, market psychology plays a significant role in determining the direction of price movements. Traders who follow the mean reversion strategy aim to exploit these psychological biases by buying assets that are trading below their historical averages and selling assets that are trading above their historical averages.

There are several different ways that traders can implement the mean reversion strategy in their trading. One common approach is to use technical indicators to identify assets that are trading at extreme levels relative to their historical averages. For example, traders may use moving averages, Bollinger Bands, or RSI indicators to identify assets that are overbought or oversold and likely to revert back towards their mean.

Another approach to mean reversion trading is to use statistical models to identify assets that are trading at extreme levels relative to their historical averages. For example, traders may use regression analysis or

114

cointegration models to identify assets that are mispriced relative to their historical relationships with other assets. By identifying these mispriced assets, traders can take advantage of temporary price discrepancies and generate profits as prices revert back to their mean.

One of the key challenges of mean reversion trading is identifying assets that are truly mispriced and not just experiencing temporary fluctuations in price. Traders must be able to distinguish between temporary price movements that are driven by market noise and true mispricings that are likely to revert back towards their mean. This requires a deep understanding of the underlying fundamentals of the asset, as well as a keen awareness of market psychology and sentiment.

In addition to identifying mispriced assets, traders must also be able to manage their risk effectively when implementing the mean reversion strategy. Because prices can continue to move away from their historical averages for extended periods of time, traders must be prepared for the possibility of further price movements against their positions. This requires careful risk management and the use of stop-loss orders to limit potential losses if prices continue to move in the wrong direction.

Despite the challenges of mean reversion trading, many traders have found success using this strategy to generate consistent profits in the financial markets. By identifying assets that are trading at extreme levels relative to their historical averages and taking advantage of temporary price discrepancies, traders can capitalize on short-term price movements and generate profits as prices revert back towards their mean.

The theory of mean reversion is a popular trading strategy that is based on the idea that asset prices tend to revert to their historical averages over time. Traders who follow the mean reversion strategy aim to profit from short-term price movements that are not justified by the underlying fundamentals of the asset.

By identifying assets that are trading at extreme levels relative to their historical averages and taking advantage of temporary price discrepancies, traders can generate consistent profits in the financial markets. While mean reversion trading can be challenging, many traders have found success using this strategy to capitalize on short-term price movements and generate profits as prices revert back towards their mean.

Developing Mean Reversion Algorithms in Python - scripts

Mean reversion is a popular trading strategy that involves identifying assets that are overbought or oversold and betting on their prices returning to their average value. This strategy is based on the belief that prices tend to revert to their mean over time, making it a potentially profitable approach for traders.

Developing mean reversion algorithms in Python can be a powerful tool for traders looking to automate their trading strategies and take advantage of market inefficiencies. In this article, we will explore how to develop mean reversion algorithms in Python and provide some example scripts to help you get started.

To begin developing mean reversion algorithms in Python, we first need to understand the concept of mean reversion and how it can be applied to trading. Mean reversion is based on the idea that prices tend to fluctuate around their average value, and when prices deviate too far from this average, they are likely to revert back to it.

One common way to measure mean reversion is to use the concept of standard deviations. By calculating the standard deviation of an asset's price over a certain period, we can identify when prices are deviating significantly from their average value. When prices deviate by a certain number of standard deviations, it may be a signal that the asset is overbought or oversold and due for a reversion to the mean.

To develop a mean reversion algorithm in Python, we can start by collecting historical price data for the asset we want to trade. This data can be obtained from various sources, such as financial websites or APIs. Once we have the historical price data, we can calculate the average price and standard deviation over a certain period, such as the past 20 days.

Next, we can calculate the z-score of the asset's price, which is a measure of how many standard deviations the current price is from the average price. A high positive z-score indicates that the asset is overbought, while a low negative z-score indicates that the asset is oversold.

To develop a mean reversion trading strategy, we can set up rules based on the z-score of the asset's price. For example, we can buy the asset when the z-score is below a certain threshold, indicating that it is oversold and likely to revert to the mean. Similarly, we can sell the asset when the z-score is above a certain threshold, indicating that it is overbought and due for a reversion.

Now, let's look at an example script in Python that implements a mean reversion algorithm using the above principles:

```python
import pandas as pd import numpy as np

# Load historical price data
data = pd.read_csv('historical_data.csv')
```

```python
# Calculate the average price and standard deviation
data['mean'] = data['price'].rolling(window=20).mean()
data['std'] = data['price'].rolling(window=20).std()


# Calculate the z-score
data['z_score'] = (data['price'] - data['mean']) / data['std']

# Define trading signals
data['signal'] = np.where(data['z_score'] < -2, 1, 0)
data['signal'] = np.where(data['z_score'] > 2, -1, data['signal'])

# Calculate returns
data['returns'] = data['price'].pct_change()
data['strategy_returns'] = data['signal'].shift(1) * data['returns']

# Calculate cumulative returns
data['cumulative_strategy_returns'] = (1 + data['strategy_returns']).cumprod()

# Plot cumulative returns
data['cumulative_strategy_returns'].plot()
```

In this script, we first load the historical price data and calculate the average price and standard deviation over a 20-day period. We then calculate the z-score of the asset's price and define trading signals based on the z-score. We calculate the returns of the asset and the strategy returns based on the trading signals. Finally, we calculate the cumulative returns of the strategy and plot the results.

Developing mean reversion algorithms in Python can be a powerful tool for traders looking to automate their trading strategies and take advantage of market inefficiencies. By understanding the concept of mean reversion and how it can be applied to trading, traders can develop profitable algorithms that exploit price deviations from the mean.

mean reversion algorithms in Python can be a valuable tool for traders looking to automate their trading strategies and take advantage of market inefficiencies. By developing algorithms that identify overbought and oversold assets and bet on their prices reverting to the mean, traders can potentially achieve profitable results.

By following the example script provided in this article and experimenting with different parameters and assets, traders can develop mean reversion algorithms that suit their trading style and risk tolerance.

Chapter 11: Arbitrage Strategies in trading

Arbitrage is a trading strategy that involves taking advantage of price discrepancies in different markets to make a profit. In this chapter, we will discuss the various arbitrage strategies that traders can use to capitalize on theseopportunities.

One of the most common forms of arbitrage is known as "riskless arbitrage." This strategy involves buying an asset in one market and selling it in another market where the price is higher. By doing this, traders can lock in a profit without taking on any risk. For example, if a stock is trading at $50 on the New York Stock Exchange and $52 on the London Stock Exchange, a trader could buy the stock in New York and sell it in London to make a $2 profit per share.

Another form of arbitrage is known as "statistical arbitrage." This strategy involves identifying mispricings in related securities and taking advantage of them. For example, if two stocks are highly correlated but one is trading at a lower price than the other, a trader could buy the undervalued stock and short sell the overvalued stock to profit from the price convergence.

Arbitrage can also be done in the foreign exchange market, where traders can take advantage of differences in exchange rates between different currencies. For example, if the exchange rate between the US dollar and the

Japanese yen is 100:1 in the US market and 105:1 in the Japanese market, a trader could buy dollars in the US market and sell them in the Japanese market to make a profit.

In addition to traditional arbitrage strategies, there are also more complex forms of arbitrage that involve derivatives. For example, traders can use options to create arbitrage opportunities by exploiting discrepancies between the prices of options and the underlying assets. By buying a call option and selling a put option on the same underlying asset, traders can lock in a profit regardless of which way the price moves.

Arbitrage strategies can be highly profitable, but they also come with risks. One of the biggest risks of arbitrage is that the price discrepancies that traders are exploiting may not last long enough for them to make a profit. In fast-moving markets, prices can change rapidly, making it difficult to execute arbitrage trades before the opportunity disappears.

Another risk of arbitrage is that it requires significant capital to execute. In order to take advantage of price discrepancies, traders need to have enough funds to buy and sell assets in different markets simultaneously. This can be a barrier for smaller traders who may not have the resources to engage in arbitrage.

Despite these risks, many traders continue to use arbitrage strategies because of the potential for high returns. By carefully monitoring market prices and executing trades quickly, traders can capitalize on price discrepancies and generate profits with minimal risk.

Understanding Arbitrage Opportunities in Trading

Arbitrage is a trading strategy that involves taking advantage of price differences in different markets or assets to make a profit. It is a common practice in the financial markets and is used by traders to exploit inefficiencies in pricing. Understanding arbitrage opportunities can be a lucrative way to make money in trading, but it requires a good understanding of the markets and the ability to act quickly.

There are several types of arbitrage opportunities that traders can take advantage of, including:

Price arbitrage: This is the most common type of arbitrage, where traders buy an asset in one market and sell it in another market where the price is higher. For example, if a stock is trading at $50 in one market and $55 in another market, a trader can buy the stock in the first market and sell it in the second market to make a profit.

Currency arbitrage: This type of arbitrage involves taking advantage of differences in exchange rates between different currencies. Traders can buy a currency in one market where it is undervalued and sell it in another market where it is overvalued to make a profit.

Statistical arbitrage: This type of arbitrage involves using statistical models to identify mispriced assets and take advantage of the price discrepancies. Traders can use quantitative analysis and algorithms to identify arbitrage

124

opportunities in the markets.

Merger arbitrage: This type of arbitrage involves taking advantage of price discrepancies between the stock prices of companies involved in a merger or acquisition. Traders can buy the stock of the target company and short the stock of the acquiring company to profit from the price difference.

Arbitrage opportunities can arise in various markets, including stocks, bonds, currencies, commodities, and derivatives. Traders need to have a good understanding of the markets they are trading in and the factors that can influence prices to identify profitable arbitrage opportunities.

One of the key factors that can influence arbitrage opportunities is market efficiency. In efficient markets, prices quickly adjust to reflect all available information, making it difficult to find mispriced assets. However, in less efficient markets, such as emerging markets or small-cap stocks, there may be more opportunities for arbitrage.

Traders also need to consider transaction costs when trading arbitrage opportunities. Buying and selling assets in different markets can incur fees and commissions, which can eat into profits. Traders need to carefully calculate the potential profits and costs of an arbitrage opportunity to determine if it is worth pursuing.

Another important factor to consider when trading arbitrage opportunities is timing. Prices can change quickly in the markets, so traders need to act fast to take advantage of price discrepancies. This requires monitoring the markets closely and being ready to execute trades quickly when opportunities arise.

In addition to understanding the markets and factors that can influence prices, traders also need to have the right tools and technology to trade arbitrage opportunities effectively. This includes access to real-time market data, trading platforms, and algorithms that can help identify and execute trades quickly.

Overall, understanding arbitrage opportunities in trading requires a combination of market knowledge, analytical skills, and the ability to act quickly. By carefully analyzing the markets and identifying profitable opportunities, traders can potentially make significant profits through arbitrage trading. However, it is important to remember that arbitrage trading carries risks, and traders should carefully consider these risks before engaging in arbitrage strategies.

Implementing Arbitrage Strategies Using Python - scripts

Arbitrage is a trading strategy that involves taking advantage of price differences in different markets. It is a way to profit from discrepancies in the prices of assets, such as stocks, commodities, or cryptocurrencies, by buying low in one market and selling high in another.

In this article, we will discuss how to implement arbitrage strategies using Python scripts. Python is a popular programming language for data analysis and financial modeling, making it a great tool for developing and testing arbitrage strategies.

To begin, let's first understand the concept of arbitrage and how it works. Arbitrage is based on the principle of the law of one price, which states that identical goods should sell for the same price in different markets.
However, due to various factors such as supply and demand, transaction costs, and market inefficiencies, pricescan differ between markets.

Arbitrage opportunities arise when the price of an asset is mispriced in one market compared to another. Traders can exploit these price differences by buying the asset in the market where it is cheaper and selling it in the market where it is more expensive, thereby making a profit.

There are several types of arbitrage strategies, including:

Spatial arbitrage: This involves buying an asset in one

location and selling it in another location where the price is higher.

Temporal arbitrage: This involves buying an asset at a lower price and selling it at a higher price in the same market, but at different times.

Statistical arbitrage: This involves exploiting statistical relationships between assets to profit from price discrepancies.

Now, let's look at an example of how to implement a simple arbitrage strategy using Python scripts. In this example, we will focus on spatial arbitrage, where we will compare the prices of a stock in two different markets and execute trades to profit from the price difference.

First, we need to import the necessary libraries in Python, such as pandas for data manipulation and requests for fetching data from APIs. We will also need to install the ccxt library, which provides a unified API for accessing cryptocurrency exchanges.

```python
import pandas as pdimport requests import ccxt
```

Next, we need to define the function to fetch price data from two different markets. In this example, we will compare the prices of Bitcoin on two cryptocurrency exchanges, Binance and Coinbase.

```python
def get_price(exchange, symbol):
    url = f"https://api.{exchange}.com/api/v1/ticker/{symbol}"
    response = requests.get(url)
    data = response.json() price = float(data['last']) return price

binance_price = get_price('binance', 'BTCUSDT')
coinbase_price = get_price('coinbase', 'BTC-USD')

print(f"Binance price: {binance_price}") print(f"Coinbase price: {coinbase_price}")
```

After fetching the prices from both exchanges, we can calculate the price difference and execute trades if there is an arbitrage opportunity. In this example, we will assume a simple strategy where we buy Bitcoin on the exchange with the lower price and sell it on the exchange with the higher price.

```python
if binance_price < coinbase_price:
    buy_price = binance_price sell_price = coinbase_price
    profit = sell_price - buy_price
    print(f"Buy Bitcoin on Binance at {buy_price} and sell on Coinbase at {sell_price} for a profit of {profit}")else:
    buy_price = coinbase_price sell_price = binance_price
    profit = sell_price - buy_price
    print(f"Buy Bitcoin on Coinbase at {buy_price} and sell on Binance at {sell_price} for a profit of {profit}")
```

This is a basic example of how to implement an arbitrage strategy using Python scripts. However, in practice, arbitrage trading is more complex and involves factors such as transaction costs, market liquidity, and execution speed. Traders also need to consider the risks involved, such as price slippage and exchange rate fluctuations.

To develop more sophisticated arbitrage strategies, traders can use advanced techniques such as machine learning, time series analysis, and algorithmic trading. Python provides a wide range of libraries and tools for implementing these strategies, such as NumPy, SciPy, and TensorFlow.

Arbitrage is a popular trading strategy for taking advantage of price differences in different markets. By implementing arbitrage strategies using Python scripts, traders can automate the process of identifying and executing profitable trades. However, it is important to conduct thorough research and testing before deploying any arbitrage strategy in live trading.

Chapter 12: High-Frequency Trading (HFT)

High-frequency trading (HFT) is a type of trading that uses sophisticated algorithms and computer programs to execute trades at extremely high speeds. These trades are typically executed in milliseconds, allowing traders to take advantage of small price discrepancies in the market. HFT has become increasingly popular in recent years, with some estimates suggesting that it now accounts for a significant portion of all trading activity on major stock exchanges.

One of the key advantages of HFT is its speed. By using powerful computers and algorithms, HFT traders are able to execute trades much faster than human traders. This allows them to take advantage of small price discrepancies in the market before other traders can react. In some cases, HFT traders are able to make thousands of trades in a single second, giving them a significant edge over traditional traders.

Another advantage of HFT is its ability to provide liquidity to the market. By constantly buying and selling securities, HFT traders help to ensure that there is always a buyer or seller available for a particular security. This can help to reduce the impact of large trades on the market and make it easier for investors to buy and sell securities quickly.

However, HFT has also been the subject of controversy and criticism. Some critics argue that HFT can create instability in the market and lead to sudden and unpredictable price movements. They also point out that HFT can give an unfair advantage to large institutional investors who have the resources to invest in high-speed trading technology.

In response to these concerns, regulators have implemented a number of measures to try to regulate HFT. For example, some exchanges have introduced "speed bumps" that delay HFT trades by a fraction of a second in order to level the playing field for other traders. Regulators have also introduced new rules and regulations designed to increase transparency and oversight of HFT activity.

Despite these challenges, HFT continues to be a popular and profitable trading strategy for many investors. In fact, some estimates suggest that HFT accounts for as much as 50% of all trading activity on major stock exchanges. This has led to a debate about the impact of HFT on the market and whether it is ultimately beneficial or harmful to investors.

High-frequency trading is a complex and controversial trading strategy that has become increasingly popular in recent years. While HFT offers a number of advantages, including speed and liquidity, it also raises concerns about market stability and fairness. As regulators continue to grapple with these issues, it is clear that HFT will continue to be a topic of debate in the financial industry for years to come.

High-Frequency Trading Fundamentals

High-frequency trading (HFT) is a type of trading that involves the use of sophisticated algorithms and high-speed computer programs to execute trades at a rapid pace. This form of trading has become increasingly popular in recent years, as advances in technology have made it possible to execute trades in a matter of milliseconds.

One of the key principles of high-frequency trading is the concept of latency, which refers to the delay between the time a trade is initiated and the time it is executed. In high-frequency trading, even a small delay can result in a significant loss, so traders must use the fastest possible technology to minimize latency.

Another important aspect of high-frequency trading is the use of algorithms to analyze market data and identify profitable trading opportunities. These algorithms are designed to take advantage of small price discrepancies in the market and execute trades at lightning speed to capitalize on these opportunities.

High-frequency trading is often associated with large financial institutions and hedge funds, as these organizations have the resources and expertise to develop and implement complex trading strategies. However, individual traders can also participate in high-frequency trading by using specialized trading platforms and software.

One of the main advantages of high-frequency trading is its ability to generate profits quickly and consistently. By executing a large number of trades in a short period of time, high-frequency traders can take advantage of small price movements to generate significant returns.

However, high-frequency trading also comes with a number of risks. One of the main risks is the potential for market manipulation, as high-frequency traders can use their speed and technology to influence market prices in their favor. This can lead to market distortions and unfair advantages for certain traders.

Another risk of high-frequency trading is the potential for technical glitches and system failures. Because high-frequency trading relies on complex algorithms and high-speed technology, even a small error can result in significant losses. Traders must therefore be vigilant in monitoring their systems and implementing safeguards to protect against technical failures.

Despite these risks, high-frequency trading continues to be a popular and profitable trading strategy for many investors. By leveraging technology and algorithms to execute trades at lightning speed, high-frequency traders can generate impressive returns in a short period of time.

In conclusion, high-frequency trading is a complex and sophisticated form of trading that involves the use of advanced technology and algorithms to execute trades at rapid speed. While high-frequency trading offers the potential for significant profits, it also comes with a number of risks that traders must be aware of. By understanding the fundamentals of high-frequency trading and implementing proper risk management strategies, traders can maximize their chances of success in this fast-paced and dynamic market.

Building Scalping Algorithms in Python - scripts

Scalping is a trading strategy that involves making small profits on a large number of trades throughout the day. It requires a high level of precision and speed, as scalpers aim to capitalize on small price movements in the market. Building scalping algorithms in Python can help traders automate this strategy and execute trades quickly and efficiently.

In this article, we will provide an example of a scalping algorithm in Python using scripts. We will walk through the process of building the algorithm step by step, from importing libraries to defining trading rules and executing trades. By the end of this article, you will have a basic understanding of how to create a scalping algorithm in Python and how to implement it in your trading strategy.

Step 1: Importing Libraries

The first step in building a scalping algorithm in Python is to import the necessary libraries. We will be using the pandas library for data manipulation, the numpy library for numerical operations, and the ccxt library for accessing cryptocurrency exchange data. You can install these libraries using the following commands:

```python
pip install pandaspip install numpypip install ccxt
```

Once you have installed the libraries, you can import them

into your Python script as follows:

```python
import pandas as pd import numpy as np import ccxt
```

Step 2: Initializing the Exchange

Next, we need to initialize the exchange that we will be using to access market data and execute trades. In this example, we will be using the Binance exchange. You will need to create an account on Binance and generate API keys to access the exchange data. Once you have your API keys, you can initialize the exchange in your Python script as follows:

```python
exchange = ccxt.binance({ 'apiKey': 'YOUR_API_KEY',
'secret': 'YOUR_API_SECRET'
})
```

Step 3: Getting Market Data

Once we have initialized the exchange, we can start retrieving market data for the cryptocurrency pair that we want to trade. In this example, we will be using the BTC/USDT pair. You can retrieve market data using the following code:

```python
symbol = 'BTC/USDT'
ohlcv = exchange.fetch_ohlcv(symbol, timeframe='1m', limit=100)
df = pd.DataFrame(ohlcv, columns=['timestamp', 'open', 'high', 'low', 'close', 'volume']) df['timestamp'] = pd.to_datetime(df['timestamp'], unit='ms')
df.set_index('timestamp', inplace=True)
```

Step 4: Defining Trading Rules

Now that we have retrieved market data, we can define the trading rules for our scalping algorithm. In this example, we will use a simple moving average crossover strategy. We will calculate the short-term and long-term moving averages of the closing prices and generate buy and sell signals based on the crossover of these averages.

```python
df['short_ma'] = df['close'].rolling(window=5).mean()
df['long_ma'] = df['close'].rolling(window=20).mean()

df['signal'] = np.where(df['short_ma'] > df['long_ma'], 1, 0)df['position'] = df['signal'].diff()
```

Step 5: Executing Trades

Finally, we can execute trades based on the trading signals generated by our algorithm. In this example, we will buy when the short-term moving average crosses above the long-term moving average and sell when the short-term moving average crosses below the long-term moving average.

```python
for i in range(1, len(df)):
    if df['position'].iloc[i] == 1:
        exchange.create_market_buy_order(symbol, 0.001)
    elif df['position'].iloc[i] == -1:
        exchange.create_market_sell_order(symbol, 0.001)
```

Step 6: Putting It All Together

Now that we have defined our trading rules and executed trades, we can put it all together in a complete Python script. Below is the full script for our scalping algorithm:

```python
```

```python
import pandas as pd import numpy as np import ccxt

exchange = ccxt.binance({ 'apiKey': 'YOUR_API_KEY',
'secret': 'YOUR_API_SECRET'
})

symbol = 'BTC/USDT'
ohlcv = exchange.fetch_ohlcv(symbol, timeframe='1m',
limit=100)
df = pd.DataFrame(ohlcv, columns=['timestamp', 'open',
'high', 'low', 'close', 'volume']) df['timestamp'] =
pd.to_datetime(df['timestamp'], unit='ms')
df.set_index('timestamp', inplace=True)

df['short_ma'] = df['close'].rolling(window=5).mean()
df['long_ma'] = df['close'].rolling(window=20).mean()

df['signal'] = np.where(df['short_ma'] >
```

Chapter 13: Machine Learning for Trading

In recent years, machine learning has become an integral part of the financial industry, particularly in the field of trading. With the vast amount of data available in the financial markets, machine learning algorithms have proven to be highly effective in predicting market trends and making informed trading decisions. In this chapter, we will explore the various ways in which machine learning is being used in trading and how it can be leveraged to improve trading strategies.

One of the key advantages of using machine learning in trading is its ability to analyze large datasets and identify patterns that may not be readily apparent to human traders. By training algorithms on historical market data, machine learning models can learn to recognize trends and make predictions about future price movements. This can help traders make more informed decisions and increase the likelihood of making profitable trades.

There are several different types of machine learning algorithms that can be used in trading, including supervised learning, unsupervised learning, and reinforcement learning. Supervised learning involves training a model on labeled data, where the algorithm is provided with input-output pairs and learns to make predictions based on this data.

Unsupervised learning, on the other hand, involves

training a model on unlabeled data and allowing it to find patterns and relationships on its own. Reinforcement learning is a type of machine learning that involves training a model to make decisions based on feedback from its environment, such as rewards or penalties.

One of the most common applications of machine learning in trading is in the development of trading strategies. By training algorithms on historical market data, traders can create models that can predict future price movements and identify profitable trading opportunities. These models can be used to automate trading decisions, allowing traders to execute trades more quickly and efficiently.

Another application of machine learning in trading is in risk management. By analyzing historical market data, machine learning algorithms can identify potential risks and help traders mitigate them. For example, algorithms can be used to calculate the optimal position size for a given trade, based on factors such as market volatility and risk tolerance. This can help traders minimize losses and maximize profits.

Machine learning can also be used to improve market analysis and forecasting. By analyzing market data in real-time, machine learning algorithms can identify trends and patterns that may not be apparent to human traders.
This can help traders make more accurate predictions about future market movements and adjust their trading strategies accordingly.

Overall, machine learning has the potential to

revolutionize the way trading is done in the financial markets. By leveraging the power of algorithms and data analysis, traders can make more informed decisions, minimize risks, and maximize profits. As machine learning continues to advance, we can expect to see even more innovative applications in trading, leading to more efficient and profitable trading strategies.

Machine Learning Techniques fundamentals

Machine learning techniques are a fundamental aspect of artificial intelligence that involves the development of algorithms and models that can learn from and make predictions or decisions based on data. These techniques have become increasingly important in a wide range of industries, from healthcare to finance to marketing, as they allow for more accurate and efficient analysis of large datasets.

There are several key concepts and techniques that are essential to understanding machine learning. In this article, we will explore some of the fundamentals of machine learning techniques, including supervised learning, unsupervised learning, and reinforcement learning.

Supervised learning is a type of machine learning in which the algorithm is trained on a labeled dataset. This means that each data point in the dataset is associated with a specific label or outcome. The goal of supervisedlearning is to learn a mapping from input data to output labels, so that the algorithm can make predictions or decisions on new, unseen data.

One of the most common supervised learning techniques is regression, which involves predicting a continuous outcome variable based on one or more input variables. For example, a regression model could be used to predict the price of a house based on its size, location, and other features.

Another type of supervised learning is classification, which involves predicting a categorical outcome variable. For example, a classification model could be used to predict whether an email is spam or not spam based on its content and other features.

In contrast to supervised learning, unsupervised learning involves training the algorithm on an unlabeled dataset. This means that the algorithm must discover patterns or relationships in the data without any explicit guidance. Unsupervised learning is often used for tasks such as clustering, where the goal is to group similar data points together, or dimensionality reduction, where the goal is to reduce the number of input variables while preserving as much information as possible.

One common unsupervised learning technique is k-means clustering, which involves partitioning a dataset into a specified number of clusters based on the similarity of data points. Another technique is principal component analysis (PCA), which involves finding a set of orthogonal axes that capture the most variation in the data.

Reinforcement learning is a third type of machine learning technique that involves training an agent to take actions in an environment in order to maximize a reward. Unlike supervised and unsupervised learning, reinforcement learning does not rely on labeled data but instead learns through trial and error.

One of the key concepts in reinforcement learning is the idea of an agent, which is the entity that takes actions in the environment. The agent receives feedback from the environment in the form of rewards or punishments, which it uses to learn the optimal policy for taking actions.

One common reinforcement learning technique is Q-learning, which involves learning a value function that estimates the expected future rewards for each action in each state. The agent uses this value function to select the best action to take in each state, with the goal of maximizing its cumulative reward over time.

In addition to these fundamental concepts, there are several key techniques and algorithms that are commonly used in machine learning. One of the most popular algorithms is the support vector machine (SVM), which is a supervised learning algorithm that is used for classification and regression tasks.

Another popular algorithm is the random forest, which is an ensemble learning technique that combines multiple decision trees to make more accurate predictions. Random forests are often used for tasks such as image classification and fraud detection.

Deep learning is another important area of machine learning that involves training neural networks with multiple layers of interconnected nodes. Deep learning has been particularly successful in tasks such as image recognition, natural language processing, and speech recognition.

One of the key advantages of deep learning is its ability to automatically learn features from raw data, which can be particularly useful for tasks where manually engineered features are difficult to define. For example, in image recognition, deep learning models can learn to recognize patterns and objects in images without the need for handcrafted features.

In addition to these techniques, there are several best practices and considerations that are important to keep in mind when working with machine learning. One important consideration is the bias and fairness of machine learning models, as algorithms can inadvertently perpetuate or amplify existing biases in the data.

It is important to carefully evaluate the training data to ensure that it is representative and unbiased, and to monitor the performance of the model on different subgroups to detect any disparities. Additionally, it is important to consider the interpretability of machine learning models, as complex models such as deep neural networks can be difficult to understand and explain.

Machine learning techniques are a fundamental aspect of artificial intelligence that involves the development of algorithms and models that can learn from and make predictions or decisions based on data. There are several key concepts and techniques that are essential to understanding machine learning, including supervised learning, unsupervised learning, and reinforcement learning.

Implementing Machine Learning Models for Trading in python - scripts

Implementing machine learning models for trading in Python can be a powerful tool for investors looking to make data-driven decisions in the financial markets. By using historical data to train models, traders can identify patterns and trends that can help them predict future price movements and make more informed trading decisions.

There are many different machine learning models that can be used for trading, including regression models, classification models, and clustering models. Each type of model has its own strengths and weaknesses, and the best model to use will depend on the specific trading strategy being employed.

One popular machine learning model for trading is the random forest model. Random forests are a type of ensemble learning method that combines multiple decision trees to create a more accurate and robust model. Random forests are particularly well-suited for trading because they can handle large amounts of data and are less prone to overfitting than other types of models.

To implement a random forest model for trading in Python, first you will need to import the necessary libraries. This includes the pandas library for working with data, the scikit-learn library for building machine learning models, and the matplotlib library for visualizing data.

```python
import pandas as pd
from sklearn.ensemble import RandomForestClassifier
from sklearn.model_selection import train_test_split
from sklearn.metrics import accuracy_score
import matplotlib.pyplot as plt
```

Next, you will need to import your historical trading data into a pandas DataFrame. This data should include features that you believe are relevant for predicting future price movements, such as price data, volume data, and technical indicators.

```python
data = pd.read_csv('trading_data.csv')
```

Once you have imported your data, you will need to preprocess it before training your model. This may involve normalizing the data, handling missing values, and encoding categorical variables. For example, you can normalize your data using the MinMaxScaler from scikit-learn.

```python
from sklearn.preprocessing import MinMaxScaler

scaler = MinMaxScaler()
data_normalized = scaler.fit_transform(data)
```

Next, you will need to split your data into training and testing sets. This will allow you to train your model on a portion of the data and then evaluate its performance on unseen data. You can use the train_test_split function from scikit-learn to do this.

```python
X = data_normalized.drop('target_variable', axis=1) y = data_normalized['target_variable']

X_train, X_test, y_train, y_test = train_test_split(X, y, test_size=0.2, random_state=42)
```

Now that you have preprocessed your data and split it into training and testing sets, you can train your random forest model. To do this, you will need to create an instance of the RandomForestClassifier class from scikit-learn and fit it to your training data.

```python
rf = RandomForestClassifier(n_estimators=100, random_state=42)rf.fit(X_train, y_train)
```

Once your model has been trained, you can use it to make predictions on your testing data and evaluate its performance. You can use the predict method to generate predictions and then use the accuracy_score function from scikit-learn to calculate the accuracy of your model.

```python
predictions = rf.predict(X_test)
```

```
accuracy    =    accuracy_score(y_test,    predictions)
print(f'Accuracy: {accuracy}')
```

Finally, you can visualize the performance of your model using a confusion matrix. This will allow you to see how well your model is performing in terms of true positives, true negatives, false positives, and false negatives.

```python
from sklearn.metrics import confusion_matrix

conf_matrix = confusion_matrix(y_test, predictions)
plt.matshow(conf_matrix, cmap='Blues') plt.colorbar()
plt.xlabel('Predicted')plt.ylabel('Actual') plt.show()
```

Implementing machine learning models for trading in Python can be a powerful tool for investors looking to make data-driven decisions in the financial markets. By using historical data to train models, traders can identify patterns and trends that can help them predict future price movements and make more informed trading decisions. The random forest model is just one example of a machine learning model that can be used for trading, and there are many other models and techniques that can be explored.

By following the steps outlined in this article, you can start building and testing machine learning models for trading in Python and take your trading strategy to the next level.

Chapter 14: Time Series Analysis in Trading

Time series analysis is a crucial tool for traders looking to make informed decisions in the financial markets. By analyzing historical data and identifying patterns and trends, traders can gain valuable insights into potential future price movements. In this chapter, we will delve into the key concepts of time series analysis and how it can be applied to trading.

One of the fundamental concepts in time series analysis is the idea of a time series, which is a sequence of data points collected at regular intervals over time. In the context of trading, a time series typically represents the price of a financial instrument, such as a stock, commodity, or currency, over a specific period. By analyzing these data points, traders can identify patterns and trends that can help them make more informed trading decisions.

There are several key components of time series analysis that traders should be familiar with. One of the most important concepts is that of trend analysis, which involves identifying and analyzing the long-term direction of a time series. By identifying trends, traders can determine whether a financial instrument is likely to increase or decrease in value over time, and adjust their trading strategies accordingly.

Another important concept in time series analysis is that of seasonality, which refers to regular and predictable patterns that occur at specific times of the year. For example, certain financial instruments may exhibit seasonal trends based on factors such as weather, holidays, or economic cycles. By understanding these seasonal patterns, traders can anticipate potential price movements and adjust their trading strategies accordingly.

In addition to trend analysis and seasonality, time series analysis also involves the concept of volatility, which refers to the degree of variation in a time series over time. High volatility can indicate that a financial instrument is experiencing rapid price movements, while low volatility may suggest that the instrument is relatively stable.
By analyzing volatility, traders can assess the level of risk associated with a particular financial instrument and adjust their trading strategies accordingly.

One of the key tools used in time series analysis is technical analysis, which involves using statistical techniques to analyze historical price data and identify patterns and trends. Technical analysis can help traders identify potential entry and exit points for trades, as well as determine the likelihood of future price movements. By combining technical analysis with other forms of analysis, such as fundamental analysis and sentiment analysis, traders can gain a more comprehensive understanding of the financial markets and make more informed trading decisions.

Time series analysis is a valuable tool for traders looking to make informed decisions in the financial markets. By analyzing historical data and identifying patterns and trends, traders can gain valuable insights into potential future price movements. By understanding key concepts such as trend analysis, seasonality, and volatility, traders can develop more effective trading strategies and improve their overall trading performance. By incorporating time series analysis into their trading toolkit, traders can increase their chances of success in the competitive world of trading.

Techniques for Time Series Forecasting

Time series forecasting is a crucial aspect of data analysis that involves predicting future values based on historical data. This technique is widely used in various industries such as finance, healthcare, retail, and manufacturing to make informed decisions and improve business processes. In this article, we will discuss some of the most commonly used techniques for time series forecasting and how they can be implemented in differentscenarios.

Autoregressive Integrated Moving Average (ARIMA):

ARIMA is a popular time series forecasting technique that combines autoregressive (AR), integrated (I), and moving average (MA) components to model and predict future values. The AR component captures the linear relationship between an observation and its lagged values, the MA component models the error term as a linear combination of past error terms, and the I component accounts for the trend in the data by differencing the series.

To implement ARIMA, the first step is to identify the optimal values for the p, d, and q parameters, which represent the number of lagged observations, the degree of differencing, and the number of lagged forecast errors, respectively. This can be done using techniques such as autocorrelation and partial autocorrelation plots, as well as the Akaike Information Criterion (AIC) and Bayesian Information Criterion (BIC) to compare different model specifications.

155

Once the parameters are determined, the ARIMA model can be trained on the historical data and used to make forecasts for future time periods. The model can be evaluated using metrics such as mean absolute error (MAE), mean squared error (MSE), and root mean squared error (RMSE) to assess its accuracy and reliability.

Seasonal Autoregressive Integrated Moving Average (SARIMA):
SARIMA is an extension of the ARIMA model that incorporates seasonal components to capture periodic patterns in the data. In addition to the p, d, and q parameters, SARIMA models also include seasonal parameters (P, D, Q) that represent the seasonal autoregressive, differencing, and moving average components.

To implement SARIMA, the seasonal parameters must be identified along with the non-seasonal parameters using the same techniques as for ARIMA. The model can then be trained and evaluated in the same way as ARIMA, with the addition of seasonal metrics such as seasonal MAE and seasonal RMSE to assess its performance.

SARIMA is particularly useful for time series data that exhibit strong seasonal patterns, such as sales data that follow a yearly or quarterly cycle. By incorporating seasonal components into the model, SARIMA can provide more accurate and reliable forecasts for seasonal time series data.

Exponential Smoothing (ES):
Exponential smoothing is a simple yet effective time series

forecasting technique that assigns exponentially decreasing weights to past observations to capture trends and seasonality in the data. There are several variations of exponential smoothing models, including simple exponential smoothing (SES), double exponential smoothing (DES), and triple exponential smoothing (TES) or Holt-Winters method.

SES is the most basic form of exponential smoothing that assigns equal weights to all past observations and is suitable for data with no clear trend or seasonality. DES extends SES by incorporating a trend component to capture linear trends in the data, while TES adds a seasonal component to account for periodic patterns.

To implement exponential smoothing, the smoothing parameter (alpha) must be determined, which controls the rate at which past observations are discounted. The optimal value of alpha can be selected using techniques such as grid search or cross-validation to minimize the forecasting error.

Exponential smoothing models can be trained on historical data and used to make forecasts for future time periods. The models can be evaluated using metrics such as mean absolute percentage error (MAPE) and symmetric mean absolute percentage error (SMAPE) to assess their accuracy and reliability.

Seasonal Decomposition of Time Series (STL):
STL is a time series decomposition technique that separates a time series into its seasonal, trend, and residual components to analyze and forecast each

component separately. The seasonal component captures periodic patterns in the data, the trend component represents the long-term movement, and the residual component accounts for random fluctuations.

To implement STL, the time series data is decomposed using a seasonal-trend decomposition procedure based on LOESS (STL) algorithm, which iteratively decomposes the data into its seasonal, trend, and residual components. The components can then be modeled and forecasted individually using techniques such as ARIMA or exponential smoothing.

STL is particularly useful for time series data that exhibit complex seasonal patterns or trends, as it allows for a more detailed analysis and forecasting of each component. By decomposing the data into its constituent parts, STL can provide more accurate and reliable forecasts for time series data with multiple underlying patterns.

Applying Time Series Models to Market Data in python - scripts

Time series analysis is a powerful tool for analyzing and forecasting market data. By applying time series models to market data, traders and investors can gain valuable insights into the behavior of financial markets and make more informed decisions.

Python is a popular programming language for time series analysis, thanks to its extensive libraries and tools for data manipulation and visualization. In this article, we will explore how to apply time series models to market data using Python, with examples of scripts that demonstrate the process.

Importing Market Data

The first step in applying time series models to market data is to import the data into Python. There are several ways to do this, depending on the source of the data. For example, you can use the pandas library to read data from a CSV file or connect to a database to retrieve market data.

```python
import pandas as pd

# Read market data from a CSV file market_data =
pd.read_csv('market_data.csv')

# Display the first few rows of the data
print(market_data.head())
```

```
```

Preprocessing Market Data

Before applying time series models to market data, it is important to preprocess the data to ensure that it is in the right format. This may involve cleaning the data, handling missing values, and transforming the data into a time series format.

```python
# Clean the data by removing any missing values
market_data.dropna(inplace=True)

# Convert the date column to a datetime format
market_data['date']                      =
pd.to_datetime(market_data['date'])

# Set the date column as the index of the data
market_data.set_index('date', inplace=True)

# Display the preprocessed dataprint(market_data.head())
```

Visualizing Market Data

Visualizing market data is an important step in understanding the behavior of financial markets. By plotting the data, you can identify trends, patterns, and anomalies that may be useful for building time series models.

```python
import matplotlib.pyplot as plt

# Plot the closing price of the market data
plt.figure(figsize=(12, 6)) plt.plot(market_data['close'])
plt.title('Market Data - Closing Price') plt.xlabel('Date')
plt.ylabel('Closing Price') plt.show()
```

Building Time Series Models

There are several time series models that can be applied to market data, depending on the characteristics of the data and the forecasting goals. Some common time series models include ARIMA (AutoRegressive Integrated Moving Average), SARIMA (Seasonal ARIMA), and LSTM (Long Short-Term Memory).

```python
from statsmodels.tsa.arima.model import ARIMA

# Fit an ARIMA model to the market data
model = ARIMA(market_data['close'], order=(1, 1, 1))
result = model.fit()

# Display the summary of the model
print(result.summary())
```

```
```

Forecasting Market Data

Once a time series model has been built, you can use it to forecast future values of the market data. This can help traders and investors make informed decisions about buying or selling assets based on the predicted trends.

```python
# Forecast future values of the market data forecast = result.forecast(steps=30)

# Plot the forecasted values plt.figure(figsize=(12, 6))
plt.plot(market_data['close'],       label='Actual       Data')
plt.plot(forecast, label='Forecasted Data') plt.title('Market Data - Forecasting')


plt.xlabel('Date') plt.ylabel('Closing Price') plt.legend()
plt.show()
```

Evaluating Time Series Models

It is important to evaluate the performance of time series models to ensure that they are accurate and reliable for forecasting market data. Common metrics for evaluating time series models include Mean Absolute Error (MAE), Mean Squared Error (MSE), and Root Mean Squared Error (RMSE).

```python
```

162

```
from sklearn.metrics import mean_squared_error

# Calculate the Mean Squared Error of the forecast
mse = mean_squared_error(market_data['close'][-30:],
forecast)print('Mean Squared Error:', mse)
``` Conclusion
```

In this article, we have explored how to apply time series models to market data using Python. By importing market data, preprocessing the data, building time series models, and forecasting future values, traders and investors can gain valuable insights into the behavior of financial markets and make more informed decisions.

Python provides a powerful platform for time series analysis, with its extensive libraries and tools for data manipulation and visualization. By following the examples of scripts provided in this article, you can start applying time series models to market data in Python and unlock the potential for better decision-making in the financial markets.
```

Chapter 15: Building Robust Trading Systems

We will discuss the importance of building robust trading systems for successful trading in the financial markets. A robust trading system is one that can adapt to changing market conditions and continue to generate profits over the long term. We will explore the key components of a robust trading system, including risk management, strategy development, and backtesting.

Risk management is a crucial aspect of building a robust trading system. Without proper risk management, even the most profitable trading strategy can lead to significant losses. Traders must carefully consider their risk tolerance and set appropriate stop-loss levels to protect their capital. Additionally, diversification is essential to reduce the impact of any single trade on the overall portfolio. By spreading risk across multiple trades and asset classes, traders can minimize the impact of any individual loss.

Strategy development is another critical component of building a robust trading system. Traders must carefully research and test different trading strategies to find one that fits their trading style and risk tolerance. A successful trading strategy should have a clear set of rules for entering and exiting trades, as well as guidelines for managing risk. Traders should also consider the market conditions in which their strategy performs best and adjust their approach accordingly.

Backtesting is an essential tool for evaluating the effectiveness of a trading strategy and identifying potential weaknesses. By testing a strategy against historical market data, traders can assess its performance and make any necessary adjustments before risking real capital. Backtesting can help traders identify patterns and trends in the market that may affect the success of their strategy, as well as refine their entry and exit signals.

In addition to risk management, strategy development, and backtesting, traders should also consider the importance of discipline and patience in building a robust trading system. Emotions such as fear and greed can cloud judgment and lead to impulsive trading decisions that can result in significant losses. By sticking to a well-defined trading plan and maintaining a disciplined approach, traders can avoid emotional pitfalls and stay focused on their long-term goals.

Furthermore, traders should continuously monitor and evaluate their trading system to ensure its effectiveness and adaptability to changing market conditions. By keeping detailed records of their trades and performance metrics, traders can identify areas for improvement and make necessary adjustments to their strategy. Regularly reviewing and updating their trading system will help traders stay ahead of the curve and maintain a competitive edge in the market.

In conclusion, building a robust trading system is essential for long-term success in the financial markets. By incorporating risk management, strategy development, backtesting, discipline, and patience into their trading approach, traders can increase their chances of generating consistent profits and achieving their financial goals

Designing a Trading System Architecture

Designing a trading system architecture is a complex and critical process that requires careful planning and consideration of various factors. A trading system architecture is essentially the framework that supports the execution of trading strategies and the processing of financial transactions. It is crucial for ensuring the reliability, scalability, and performance of a trading system.

When designing a trading system architecture, it is important to consider the following key components:

Data Management: Data is the lifeblood of any trading system, and effective data management is essential for ensuring the accuracy and reliability of trading decisions. This includes collecting, storing, and processing market data, order data, and trade data in real-time. It is important to have a robust data management system that can handle large volumes of data and provide fast access to relevant information.

Order Management: Order management is another critical component of a trading system architecture. This involves managing the lifecycle of orders, including order routing, order execution, and order status tracking. It is important to have a flexible and efficient order management system that can handle different types of ordersand execute trades quickly and accurately.

Risk Management: Risk management is a key concern for

any trading system, as it involves identifying, assessing, and mitigating risks associated with trading activities. This includes market risk, credit risk, operational risk, and compliance risk. A robust risk management system is essential for protecting the firm's capital and ensuring regulatory compliance.

Algorithmic Trading: Algorithmic trading is a key feature of modern trading systems, as it allows traders to execute complex trading strategies automatically. This involves developing and implementing algorithms that can analyze market data, identify trading opportunities, and execute trades in real-time. It is important to have a flexible and scalable algorithmic trading system that can adapt to changing market conditions.

Connectivity: Connectivity is another critical component of a trading system architecture, as it involves connecting to various markets, brokers, and trading venues. This includes establishing reliable and low-latency connections to ensure fast and efficient order execution. It is important to have a robust connectivity infrastructure that can handle high volumes of data and provide fast access to trading venues.

Performance Monitoring: Performance monitoring is essential for evaluating the effectiveness of a trading system architecture and identifying areas for improvement. This involves monitoring key performance metrics, such as latency, throughput, and order completion rates. It is important to have a comprehensive monitoring system that can provide real-time insights into the performance of the trading system.

Compliance and Regulation: Compliance and regulation are key considerations for designing a trading system architecture, as financial markets are highly regulated and subject to strict compliance requirements. This includes ensuring that the trading system complies with relevant regulations, such as MiFID II and GDPR. It is important to have a compliance framework that can monitor and enforce regulatory requirements.

Designing a trading system architecture is a complex and challenging process that requires careful planning and consideration of various factors. By focusing on key components such as data management, order management, risk management, algorithmic trading, connectivity, performance monitoring, and compliance, firms can build a robust and reliable trading system architecture that can support their trading activities effectively.

Integrating Algorithms with Market Data Feeds in python - scripts

In today's fast-paced financial markets, the ability to quickly analyze and act on market data is crucial for success. Algorithms have become an essential tool for traders and investors, allowing them to automate their trading strategies and make informed decisions based on real-time market data. Python has emerged as a popular programming language for developing algorithms due to its simplicity, flexibility, and extensive library support.

Integrating algorithms with market data feeds in Python can provide traders with a competitive edge by enabling them to react to market movements in real-time. By combining algorithmic trading strategies with market data feeds, traders can automate their trading decisions and execute trades more efficiently. In this article, we will explore how to integrate algorithms with market data feeds in Python using scripts as examples.

Market data feeds provide traders with real-time information on market prices, volumes, and other relevant data. These feeds are typically provided by financial data providers such as Bloomberg, Reuters, or Quandl. By integrating market data feeds into their algorithms, traders can access up-to-date information and make more informed trading decisions.

To integrate market data feeds with algorithms in Python, traders can use libraries such as pandas, numpy, and matplotlib to handle and analyze the data. These libraries provide powerful tools for data manipulation, analysis, and visualization, making it easier for traders to extract insights from market data.

One common approach to integrating market data feeds with algorithms is to create a script that continuously fetches data from the market data feed and processes it using algorithms. For example, a simple script could fetch real-time stock prices from a data provider and use a moving average algorithm to generate trading signals.

```python
import pandas as pdimport numpy as np
import matplotlib.pyplot as plt

# Fetch market data
def fetch_market_data(symbol):
# Code to fetch market data goes herereturn market_data

# Moving average algorithm
def moving_average(data, window):
return  data['Close'].rolling(window=window).mean()

# Main script
if____name_== '__main_':
symbol = 'AAPL'
market_data = fetch_market_data(symbol)

# Calculate moving averages
market_data['MA_50'] = moving_average(market_data, 50)          market_data['MA_200']          = moving_average(market_data, 200)
```

```python
# Plot moving averages plt.figure(figsize=(10, 6))
plt.plot(market_data['Close'],       label='Close       Price')
plt.plot(market_data['MA_50'],       label='50-day     MA')
plt.plot(market_data['MA_200'],      label='200-day    MA')
plt.legend()
plt.show()
```

In this script, the `fetch_market_data` function is used to fetch market data for a given stock symbol. The `moving_average` function calculates the moving averages of the stock's closing prices using a specified window size. The main script fetches market data for the stock symbol 'AAPL', calculates the 50-day and 200-day moving averages, and plots the results using matplotlib.

By running this script regularly, traders can monitor the moving averages of a stock and use them to make trading decisions. For example, if the 50-day moving average crosses above the 200-day moving average, it may signal a bullish trend, prompting traders to buy the stock.

In addition to simple moving averages, traders can implement more sophisticated algorithms to analyze market data and generate trading signals. For example, traders can use machine learning algorithms such as support vector machines or random forests to predict stock price movements based on historical data.

```python
from sklearn.svm import SVR
from sklearn.ensemble import RandomForestRegressor
from sklearn.model_selection import train_test_split
```

```python
from sklearn.metrics import mean_squared_error

# Machine learning algorithm
def machine_learning_algorithm(data):
X = data[['Open', 'High', 'Low', 'Volume']]y = data['Close']
X_train, X_test, y_train, y_test = train_test_split(X, y,
test_size=0.2, random_state=0) # Support Vector
Machine
svr = SVR(kernel='rbf')
svr.fit(X_train, y_train)    svr_predictions    =
svr.predict(X_test)

# Random Forest
rf    =    RandomForestRegressor(n_estimators=100)
rf.fit(X_train, y_train)
rf_predictions    =    rf.predict(X_test)    return
svr_predictions, rf_predictions

# Main script
if____name_== '__main_':
symbol = 'AAPL'
market_data = fetch_market_data(symbol)

# Calculate machine learning predictions
svr_predictions,    rf_predictions    =
machine_learning_algorithm(market_data)

# Evaluate predictions
svr_mse = mean_squared_error(y_test, svr_predictions)
rf_mse = mean_squared_error(y_test, rf_predictions)
```

Chapter 16: Risk Management Techniques in Trading

Risk management is a crucial aspect of trading that every trader must master in order to be successful in the financial markets. In this chapter, we will discuss some of the key risk management techniques that traders can use to protect their capital and maximize their potential for profits.

One of the most important risk management techniques in trading is setting stop-loss orders. A stop-loss order is a predetermined price level at which a trader will exit a trade to limit their losses. By setting a stop-loss order, traders can protect themselves from large losses in case the market moves against them. It is important for traders to set stop-loss orders at levels that are based on their risk tolerance and trading strategy.

Another important risk management technique is diversification. Diversification involves spreading out your investments across different asset classes, sectors, and markets to reduce the overall risk in your portfolio. By diversifying your investments, you can protect yourself from the impact of a single market event or economic downturn. Diversification can also help you take advantage of opportunities in different markets and sectors.

Position sizing is another key risk management technique that traders can use to manage their risk exposure.

174

Position sizing involves determining the amount of capital to allocate to each trade based on the risk of the trade and the trader's overall risk tolerance. By properly sizing their positions, traders can limit their losses and maximize their potential for profits.

Risk management techniques also include using leverage wisely. Leverage allows traders to control a larger position with a smaller amount of capital, but it also increases the potential for losses. Traders should use leverage cautiously and only when they have a clear understanding of the risks involved. It is important for traders to have a solid risk management plan in place before using leverage to ensure that they can protect theircapital.

Risk management techniques also include using risk-reward ratios to evaluate potential trades. A risk-reward ratio is a measure of the potential profit compared to the potential loss of a trade. By analyzing the risk-reward ratio of a trade, traders can determine whether the trade is worth taking based on their risk tolerance and trading strategy. Traders should strive to take trades with a favorable risk-reward ratio to maximize their potential for profits.

In addition to these risk management techniques, traders can also use hedging strategies to protect their capital from market volatility. Hedging involves taking an offsetting position in a related asset to reduce the risk of a trade. By using hedging strategies, traders can protect themselves from adverse market movements and limit their losses.

Overall, risk management is a critical aspect of trading

that every trader must master to be successful in the financial markets. By using stop-loss orders, diversification, position sizing, leverage, risk-reward ratios, and hedging strategies, traders can protect their capital and maximize their potential for profits. It is important for traders to develop a solid risk management plan and stick to it consistently to achieve long-term success in trading.

Principles of Risk Management in Trading

Risk management is a crucial aspect of trading in any financial market. It involves identifying, assessing, and mitigating potential risks that could impact the profitability of a trading strategy. By implementing effective risk management principles, traders can protect their capital, minimize losses, and increase the likelihood of long-term success.

There are several key principles of risk management that traders should follow to ensure they are adequately managing their risk exposure. These principles include setting stop-loss orders, diversifying their portfolio, using proper position sizing, and managing leverage effectively.

One of the most important risk management principles in trading is setting stop-loss orders. A stop-loss order is a predetermined price at which a trader will exit a trade to limit potential losses. By setting stop-loss orders, traders can protect their capital and prevent large drawdowns in their account. It is essential to set stop-loss orders at levels that are based on technical analysis and market conditions to ensure they are effective in managing risk.

Another key principle of risk management is diversifying a trading portfolio. Diversification involves spreading risk across different assets, markets, and trading strategies to reduce the impact of a single event on the overall portfolio. By diversifying their portfolio, traders can minimize the risk of significant losses and increase the likelihood of consistent profits over time.

Proper position sizing is also a critical risk management principle that traders should follow. Position sizing refers to the amount of capital that a trader allocates to each trade based on their risk tolerance and trading strategy. By using proper position sizing, traders can limit the impact of individual trades on their overall portfolio and avoid overexposure to any single position.

Managing leverage effectively is another important risk management principle in trading. Leverage allows traders to control larger positions with a smaller amount of capital, but it also increases the potential for significant losses. By using leverage responsibly and avoiding excessive risk, traders can protect their capital and avoid margin calls that could lead to account liquidation.

In addition to these key principles, traders should also consider other risk management techniques, such as setting profit targets, using trailing stops, and monitoring market volatility. By implementing a comprehensive risk management strategy that incorporates these principles, traders can protect their capital, minimize losses, and increase the likelihood of long-term success in the financial markets.

It is essential for traders to understand that trading involves inherent risks, and no strategy can guarantee profits. However, by following sound risk management principles and implementing a disciplined approach to trading, traders can increase their chances of success and achieve their financial goals.

Risk management is a critical aspect of trading that all traders should prioritize. By following key principles such as setting stop-loss orders, diversifying their portfolio, using proper position sizing, and managing leverage effectively, traders can protect their capital, minimize losses, and increase the likelihood of long-term success.

By implementing a comprehensive risk management strategy and maintaining discipline in their trading approach, traders can navigate the challenges of the financial markets and achieve their trading goals.

Implementing Risk Controls in Trading Algorithms in python - scripts

Implementing risk controls in trading algorithms is crucial for ensuring the long-term success and sustainability of a trading strategy. By incorporating risk controls into your trading algorithms, you can protect your capital from excessive losses and minimize the impact of market volatility on your portfolio. In this article, we will discuss the importance of risk controls in trading algorithms and provide examples of how to implement them using Python scripts.

Risk controls are essential for managing the inherent risks associated with trading financial markets. Without proper risk management, traders are exposed to the possibility of significant losses that can wipe out their capital and jeopardize their trading career. By implementing risk controls in trading algorithms, traders can limit their exposure to risk and protect their capital from adverse market conditions.

There are several types of risk controls that traders can incorporate into their trading algorithms, including stop-loss orders, position sizing, and risk limits. Stop-loss orders are used to automatically exit a trade when a certain price level is reached, limiting the potential losses on a trade. Position sizing refers to the amount of capital allocated to each trade, with the goal of limiting the impact of any single trade on the overall portfolio. Risk limits set the maximum amount of risk that a trader is willing to take on any given trade, helping to prevent excessive losses.

To implement risk controls in trading algorithms, traders can use programming languages such as Python to write scripts that automate the risk management process. Python is a popular programming language among traders due to its simplicity and flexibility, making it an ideal choice for developing trading algorithms. Below are examples of Python scripts that demonstrate how to implement risk controls in trading algorithms.

Example 1: Stop-loss Order

```python
import pandas as pd

def stop_loss(data, stop_loss_level):
data['stop_loss'] = data['close'] * (1 - stop_loss_level)
data['exit_price'] = data[['close', 'stop_loss']].min(axis=1)
return data

# Load historical price data
data = pd.read_csv('historical_data.csv')

# Set stop-loss level stop_loss_level = 0.05

# Implement stop-loss order
data = stop_loss(data, stop_loss_level)

print(data)
```

In this example, we define a function `stop_loss` that

calculates the stop-loss level for each data point in a historical price dataset. The function takes two arguments: the historical price data and the stop-loss level. The function calculates the stop-loss price for each data point as 5% below the closing price and assigns it to the `stop_loss` column. It then calculates the exit price as the minimum of the closing price and the stop-loss price and assigns it to the `exit_price` column.

Example 2: Position Sizing

```python
def position_sizing(data, risk_per_trade):
data['position_size'] = risk_per_trade / (data['close'] - data['stop_loss'])return data

# Set risk per trade risk_per_trade = 1000

# Implement position sizing
data = position_sizing(data, risk_per_trade)

print(data)
```

In this example, we define a function `position_sizing` that calculates the position size for each data point in a historical price dataset. The function takes two arguments: the historical price data and the risk per trade. The function calculates the position size for each data point based on the risk per trade and the difference between the closing price and the stop-loss price.

Example 3: Risk Limits

```python
def risk_limits(data, max_risk):
    data['risk_exposure'] = data['position_size'] * (data['close'] - data['stop_loss']) data['risk_exposure'] = data['risk_exposure'].cumsum()
    data['risk_exposure'] = data['risk_exposure'].clip(upper=max_risk)return data

# Set maximum risk exposuremax_risk = 5000

# Implement risk limits
data = risk_limits(data, max_risk)

print(data)
```

In this example, we define a function `risk_limits` that calculates the risk exposure for each data point in a historical price dataset. The function takes two arguments: the historical price data and the maximum risk exposure. The function calculates the risk exposure for each data point as the product of the position size and the difference between the closing price and the stop-loss price. It then calculates the cumulative risk exposure and clips it to the maximum risk exposure set by the trader.

By incorporating risk controls into trading algorithms, traders can effectively manage the risks associated with trading financial markets and protect their capital from excessive losses. Python scripts can be used to automate the risk management process and ensure that risk controls are consistently applied to trading strategies.

Traders can customize risk controls to suit their individual risk tolerance and trading objectives, helping to improve the overall performance and profitability of their trading algorithms.

Chapter 17: Portfolio Optimization in Trading

Portfolio optimization is a crucial aspect of trading that involves maximizing returns while minimizing risks. In this chapter, we will delve into the various strategies and techniques used in portfolio optimization to help traders make informed decisions and achieve their financial goals.

Understanding Portfolio Optimization

Portfolio optimization is the process of constructing an investment portfolio that maximizes returns while minimizing risks. This involves selecting a mix of assets that are expected to perform well in different market conditions and adjusting the portfolio weights accordingly.

The goal of portfolio optimization is to achieve the highest possible return for a given level of risk or to minimize risk for a given level of return. This is done by diversifying the portfolio across different asset classes, industries, and regions to reduce the impact of market fluctuations on the overall performance of the portfolio.

Modern Portfolio Theory

Modern Portfolio Theory (MPT) is a key concept in portfolio optimization that was developed by Harry Markowitz in the 1950s. According to MPT, the key to achieving optimal returns is to diversify the portfolio across assets with low or negative correlations. This helps to reduce the overall risk of the portfolio without sacrificing returns.

MPT uses statistical techniques to analyze the historical performance of assets and estimate their expected returns and risks. By constructing an efficient frontier, which represents the set of optimal portfolios that offer the highest return for a given level of risk, traders can identify the best mix of assets to include in their portfolio.

Asset Allocation

Asset allocation is a critical component of portfolio optimization that involves determining the optimal mix of assets to include in the portfolio. This is based on the investor's risk tolerance, investment goals, time horizon, and market conditions.

There are various asset classes to consider when optimizing a portfolio, including stocks, bonds, commodities, real estate, and alternative investments. Each asset class has its own risk-return profile, correlation with other assets, and market dynamics that need to be taken into account when constructing a diversified portfolio.

Risk Management

Risk management is another key aspect of portfolio optimization that involves identifying, assessing, and mitigating risks that could impact the performance of the portfolio. This includes market risk, credit risk, liquidity

186

risk, and operational risk, among others.

Traders can use various risk management techniques, such as stop-loss orders, hedging strategies, and diversification, to protect their portfolio from potential losses. By setting risk limits and monitoring the portfolio regularly, traders can ensure that their investments are aligned with their risk tolerance and financial goals.

Portfolio Rebalancing

Portfolio rebalancing is the process of adjusting the weights of assets in the portfolio to maintain the desired asset allocation and risk-return profile. This is done periodically to account for changes in market conditions, asset prices, and investor preferences.

Traders can use various rebalancing strategies, such as calendar-based rebalancing, threshold-based rebalancing, and tactical rebalancing, to ensure that their portfolio remains optimized and aligned with their investment objectives. By rebalancing the portfolio regularly, traders can take advantage of market opportunities and minimize the impact of market fluctuations on their investments.

Portfolio optimization is a critical aspect of trading that involves constructing an investment portfolio that maximizes returns while minimizing risks. By understanding the key concepts of portfolio optimization, such as Modern Portfolio Theory, asset allocation, risk management, and portfolio rebalancing, traders can make informed decisions and achieve their financial goals.

Techniques for Portfolio Optimization in Trading

Portfolio optimization is a crucial aspect of trading that involves selecting the right mix of assets to achieve the highest possible return with the lowest possible risk. By diversifying investments across a range of assets, traders can reduce their exposure to market volatility and potentially increase their overall returns. There are several techniques that traders can use to optimize their portfolios and maximize their profits.

One of the most common techniques for portfolio optimization is Modern Portfolio Theory (MPT), which was developed by Harry Markowitz in the 1950s. MPT is based on the idea that investors can achieve the highest possible return for a given level of risk by diversifying their investments across a range of assets with different levels of correlation. By combining assets that have low or negative correlations, investors can reduce the overall risk of their portfolio without sacrificing returns.

Another popular technique for portfolio optimization is the Capital Asset Pricing Model (CAPM), which was developed by William Sharpe in the 1960s. CAPM is based on the idea that the expected return on an asset is equal to the risk-free rate plus a risk premium that is proportional to the asset's beta, or sensitivity to market movements. By calculating the beta of each asset in a portfolio and weighting them accordingly, traders can optimize their portfolios to achieve the highest possible return for a given level of risk.

In addition to MPT and CAPM, traders can also use other techniques for portfolio optimization, such as mean-variance optimization, risk parity, and factor investing. Mean-variance optimization involves maximizing the expected return of a portfolio while minimizing its variance, or risk. By calculating the expected returns and variances of each asset in a portfolio and optimizing the weights accordingly, traders can achieve the highest possible return for a given level of risk.

Risk parity is another technique for portfolio optimization that involves allocating assets based on their risk contributions rather than their expected returns. By diversifying investments across assets with different levels of risk, traders can reduce the overall risk of their portfolio while potentially increasing their returns. Risk parity portfolios are typically constructed using leverage to achieve a target level of risk, which can help traders optimize their portfolios for maximum returns.

Factor investing is another popular technique for portfolio optimization that involves selecting assets based on specific factors, such as value, momentum, or quality. By constructing portfolios that are tilted towards assets with certain characteristics, traders can potentially outperform the market and achieve higher returns. Factor investing has become increasingly popular in recent years, as traders look for ways to optimize their portfolios and generate alpha.

Overall, portfolio optimization is a crucial aspect of trading that can help investors achieve the highest possible return for a given level of risk. By using techniques such as MPT, CAPM, mean-variance optimization, risk parity, and factor investing, traders can optimize their portfolios and maximize their profits. Whether you are a beginner or an experienced trader, it is essential to understand these techniques and how to apply them to your own investment strategy. By diversifying your investments, managing risk, and selecting assets based on specific factors, you can optimize your portfolio and achieve your financial goals.

Using Python for Portfolio Management in Trading - scripts

Python has become one of the most popular programming languages among traders and portfolio managers due to its flexibility, ease of use, and extensive libraries for data analysis and visualization. In this article, we will explore how Python can be used for portfolio management in trading, with examples of scripts that demonstrate its capabilities.

Python is a versatile programming language that is widely used in the financial industry for tasks such as data analysis, backtesting trading strategies, and building trading algorithms. One of the key advantages of using Python for portfolio management in trading is its ability to handle large amounts of data efficiently and to perform complex calculations quickly.

One of the most common tasks in portfolio management is the analysis of historical stock price data to identify trends and patterns that can inform investment decisions. Python provides a number of libraries, such as Pandas and NumPy, that make it easy to work with time-series data and to perform calculations such as moving averages, volatility, and correlation.

For example, let's say we have a CSV file containing historical stock price data for a portfolio of stocks. We can use the Pandas library to read the data into a DataFrame and calculate the 50-day moving average for each stock:

```python
import pandas as pd

# Read the data into a DataFrame data =
pd.read_csv('stock_data.csv')

# Calculate the 50-day moving average for each stock
data['50_day_ma']                                              =
data.groupby('stock')['price'].rolling(window=50).mean().
reset_index(0, drop=True)
```

In this script, we first import the Pandas library and read
the stock price data from a CSV file into a DataFrame. We
then use the `rolling` method to calculate the 50-day
moving average for each stock, grouping the data by the
'stock' column.

Another important aspect of portfolio management is risk
management, which involves monitoring the volatility of
the portfolio and ensuring that it is within acceptable
limits. Python provides libraries such as SciPy and
StatsModels that can be used to calculate risk metrics such
as Value at Risk (VaR) and Conditional Value at Risk
(CVaR).

For example, we can calculate the 95% VaR for a portfolio
of stocks using the historical simulation method:

```python
import numpy as np
from scipy.stats import norm
```

```
# Calculate the daily returns for each stock
data['return']                                        =
data.groupby('stock')['price'].pct_change()


# Calculate the 95% VaR for the portfolio
portfolio_returns = data.groupby('date')['return'].sum()
portfolio_volatility         =          portfolio_returns.std()
portfolio_mean_return = portfolio_returns.mean()

VaR_95    =    norm.ppf(0.05,    portfolio_mean_return,
portfolio_volatility)
```

In this script, we first calculate the daily returns for each stock by taking the percentage change in price. We then aggregate the returns for each date to calculate the daily portfolio return. Finally, we calculate the standard deviation of the portfolio returns and use the `norm.ppf` function from the SciPy library to calculate the 95% VaR.

Another important aspect of portfolio management is performance evaluation, which involves comparing the performance of the portfolio against a benchmark index or other portfolios. Python provides libraries such as Matplotlib and Seaborn that can be used to visualize the performance of the portfolio and to generate performance metrics such as Sharpe ratio and Jensen's alpha.

For example, we can plot the cumulative returns of the portfolio and a benchmark index using Matplotlib:

```python
```

```
import matplotlib.pyplot as plt

# Calculate the cumulative returns for the portfolio and
benchmark index data['cumulative_return'] = (1 +
data['return']).cumprod()
data['benchmark_cumulative_return']    =    (1    +
data['benchmark_return']).cumprod()

# Plot the cumulative returns
plt.plot(data['date'],              data['cumulative_return'],
label='Portfolio')                          plt.plot(data['date'],
data['benchmark_cumulative_return'],
label='Benchmark')plt.legend()
plt.show()
```
```

In this script, we first calculate the cumulative returns for
the portfolio and a benchmark index by taking the
cumulative product of the daily returns. We then use
Matplotlib to plot the cumulative returns over time, with
the portfolio and benchmark index shown on the same
plot.

In conclusion, Python is a powerful tool for portfolio
management in trading due to its flexibility, ease of use,
and extensive libraries for data analysis and visualization.
By using Python scripts like the examples provided in this
article, traders and portfolio managers can efficiently
analyze historical stock price data, calculate risk metrics,
and evaluate the performance of their portfolios. Whether
you are a beginner or an experienced trader, Python can
help you make more informed investment decisions and
manage your portfolio more effectively.
```

Chapter 18: Backtesting Your Strategies in Trading

Backtesting is a crucial step in the trading process that allows traders to evaluate the performance of their trading strategies using historical data. By backtesting your strategies, you can determine whether they are profitable and reliable before risking real money in the market. In this chapter, we will explore the importance of backtesting, how to conduct backtesting effectively, and the key considerations to keep in mind when backtesting your trading strategies.

Importance of Backtesting

Backtesting is essential for traders to validate their trading strategies and make informed decisions based on historical data. By backtesting your strategies, you can identify potential flaws or weaknesses in your approach and make necessary adjustments to improve your trading performance. Additionally, backtesting allows you to gain confidence in your strategies and helps you avoid costly mistakes in the live market.

Conducting Effective Backtesting

To conduct effective backtesting, it is important to follow a systematic approach and use reliable historical data. Here are some key steps to consider when backtesting your trading strategies:

Define Your Trading Strategy: Before conducting backtesting, clearly define your trading strategy, including entry and exit rules, risk management parameters, and position sizing guidelines.

Select Historical Data: Choose a reliable source of historical data that is representative of the market conditions you will be trading in. Ensure that the data is accurate and includes all relevant information such as price, volume, and market trends.

Set Up Your Backtesting Platform: Use a backtesting platform or software that allows you to simulate your trading strategy using historical data. Make sure the platform is user-friendly and provides accurate results.

Conduct Backtesting: Run your trading strategy through the backtesting platform and analyze the results. Pay attention to key performance metrics such as profitability, drawdowns, win rate, and risk-adjusted returns.

Evaluate the Results: Evaluate the performance of your trading strategy based on the backtesting results. Identify any areas of improvement or potential weaknesses in your strategy and make necessary adjustments.

Key Considerations for Backtesting

When backtesting your trading strategies, there are several key considerations to keep in mind to ensure accurate and reliable results. Here are some important factors to consider:

Data Quality: Use high-quality historical data that is accurate and free from errors. Ensure that the data is representative of the market conditions you will be trading in.

Overfitting: Avoid overfitting your trading strategy to historical data by optimizing it too much. Overfitting can lead to unrealistic performance results and may not be sustainable in the live market.

Transaction Costs: Take into account transaction costs such as commissions, slippage, and spread when conducting backtesting. These costs can have a significant impact on the profitability of your trading strategy.

Market Conditions: Consider the impact of different market conditions on your trading strategy. Test your strategy across various market environments to ensure its robustness and adaptability.

Risk Management: Incorporate effective risk management techniques into your trading strategy and evaluate their impact on performance during backtesting. Ensure that your strategy can withstand potential drawdowns and losses.

Backtesting is a valuable tool for traders to evaluate the performance of their trading strategies and make informed decisions based on historical data. By following a systematic approach, using reliable historical data, and considering key factors such as data quality, overfitting, transaction costs, market conditions, and risk management, traders can conduct effective backtesting and improve their trading performance.

Remember that backtesting is an ongoing process that requires continuous monitoring and adjustment to ensure the long-term success of your trading strategies.

Building a Backtesting Framework in Trading

Building a backtesting framework in trading is essential for any trader looking to improve their strategies and increase their chances of success in the market. Backtesting allows traders to test their trading strategies using historical data to see how they would have performed in the past. This helps traders identify strengths and weaknesses in their strategies and make necessary adjustments to improve their performance in the future.

There are several key components to consider when building a backtesting framework in trading. These include data collection, strategy development, backtesting execution, performance analysis, and optimization. By following a systematic approach to building a backtesting framework, traders can ensure that they are making informed decisions based on data-driven insights.

Data Collection

The first step in building a backtesting framework is to collect historical data for the assets you want to trade. This data can include price data, volume data, and other relevant market data. There are several sources where traders can obtain historical data, including data providers, online databases, and trading platforms.

It is important to ensure that the data collected is clean, accurate, and reliable. Traders should also consider the frequency of the data, as different timeframes can have a significant impact on the performance of trading strategies. Once the historical data is collected, it can be imported into a backtesting platform for analysis.

Strategy Development

The next step in building a backtesting framework is to develop trading strategies based on the historical data collected. Traders can use technical analysis, fundamental analysis, or a combination of both to develop their strategies. It is important to define clear entry and exit rules for each strategy, as well as risk management parameters to protect against losses.

Traders can also backtest multiple strategies simultaneously to compare their performance and identify the most profitable ones. By testing a variety of strategies, traders can gain valuable insights into which approaches work best in different market conditions.

Backtesting Execution

Once trading strategies have been developed, traders can begin the backtesting process. This involves running the strategies on historical data to see how they would have performed in the past. Traders can use backtesting platforms to automate this process and analyze the results.

During the backtesting process, traders should pay attention to key performance metrics such as profitability, drawdown, win rate, and risk-reward ratio. These metrics can help traders evaluate the effectiveness of their strategies and make informed decisions about which ones to implement in live trading.

Performance Analysis

After completing the backtesting process, traders should analyze the performance of their strategies to identify strengths and weaknesses. This can involve conducting a detailed review of the trading results, looking for patterns or trends that may indicate areas for improvement.

Traders can also use performance analysis tools to generate reports and visualizations that highlight key performance metrics. By analyzing the data, traders can gain valuable insights into the effectiveness of their strategies and make informed decisions about how to optimize their performance.

Optimization

The final step in building a backtesting framework is to optimize trading strategies based on the insights gained from performance analysis. This can involve making adjustments to entry and exit rules, risk management parameters, or other aspects of the strategies to improve their performance.

Traders can also use optimization tools to test different parameters and settings to see how they impact the performance of their strategies. By fine-tuning their strategies through optimization, traders can increase their chances of success in the market and achieve better results over time.

Building a backtesting framework in trading is a critical step for any trader looking to improve their strategies and increase their chances of success in the market. By following a systematic approach to data collection, strategy development, backtesting execution, performance analysis, and optimization, traders can make informed decisions based on data-driven insights and improve their trading performance over time.

Analyzing Backtest Results and Metrics in python - scripts

Backtesting is a crucial step in the development and evaluation of trading strategies. It involves testing a strategy on historical data to see how it would have performed in the past. Analyzing backtest results and metrics is essential for understanding the performance of a strategy and making informed decisions about its future use.

In this article, we will discuss how to analyze backtest results and metrics using Python scripts. We will cover common metrics used to evaluate trading strategies, such as Sharpe ratio, maximum drawdown, and annualized return. We will also provide examples of Python code to calculate these metrics and visualize the results.

Sharpe Ratio:

The Sharpe ratio is a measure of risk-adjusted return that takes into account the volatility of a strategy. A higher Sharpe ratio indicates better risk-adjusted performance. The formula for calculating the Sharpe ratio is:

Sharpe Ratio = (Mean Return - Risk-Free Rate) / Standard Deviation

To calculate the Sharpe ratio in Python, we can use the following code snippet:

```python
```

```python
import numpy as np

returns = np.array([0.01, 0.02, 0.03, -0.01, -0.02, 0.01])
risk_free_rate = 0.005

mean_return = np.mean(returns) std_dev = np.std(returns)
sharpe_ratio = (mean_return - risk_free_rate) / std_dev
print("Sharpe Ratio:", sharpe_ratio)
```

This code snippet calculates the Sharpe ratio for a series of returns and prints the result. You can replace the `returns` array with the actual returns of your strategy to calculate the Sharpe ratio for your backtest results. Maximum Drawdown:
Maximum drawdown is a measure of the largest loss from a peak to a trough during a specific period. It is an important metric for evaluating the downside risk of a trading strategy. The formula for calculating maximum drawdown is:

Maximum Drawdown = (Peak Value - Trough Value) / Peak Value

To calculate the maximum drawdown in Python, we can use the following code snippet:

```python
```

```python
def calculate_drawdown(returns):
peak = returns[0]drawdown = 0

for ret in returns:
if ret > peak:
peak = retelse:
drawdown = max(drawdown, (peak - ret) / peak) return drawdown
returns = np.array([0.01, 0.02, 0.03, -0.01, -0.02, 0.01])
max_drawdown       =       calculate_drawdown(returns)
print("Maximum  Drawdown:", max_drawdown)
```

This code snippet calculates the maximum drawdown for a series of returns and prints the result. You can replace the `returns` array with the actual returns of your strategy to calculate the maximum drawdown for your backtest results.

Annualized Return:

Annualized return is a measure of the average annual return of a trading strategy. It is useful for comparing the performance of different strategies over a specific period. The formula for calculating annualized return is:

Annualized Return = (1 + Total Return) ^ (1 / Number of Years) - 1

To calculate the annualized return in Python, we can use the following code snippet:

```python
```

```python
def calculate_annualized_return(returns, years):
total_return = np.prod(1 + returns) - 1 annualized_return
= (1 + total_return) ** (1 / years) - 1

return annualized_return

returns = np.array([0.01, 0.02, 0.03, -0.01, -0.02, 0.01])
years = 1
annualized_return = calculate_annualized_return(returns,
years) print("Annualized Return:", annualized_return)
```

This code snippet calculates the annualized return for a series of returns over a specific period and prints the result. You can replace the `returns` array and `years` variable with the actual returns and period of your strategy to calculate the annualized return for your backtest results.

Visualizing Backtest Results:

In addition to calculating metrics, it is also important to visualize backtest results to gain insights into the performance of a trading strategy. Python provides powerful libraries such as Matplotlib and Seaborn for creating visualizations.

For example, we can create a line plot of the cumulative returns of a strategy using Matplotlib:

```python
import matplotlib.pyplot as plt
```

```python
returns = np.array([0.01, 0.02, 0.03, -0.01, -0.02, 0.01])
cumulative_returns = np.cumprod(1 + returns) - 1
plt.plot(cumulative_returns)
plt.xlabel('Time') plt.ylabel('Cumulative Return') plt
```

Chapter 19: Simulating Trading Scenarios

In the world of trading, being able to simulate different scenarios can be a valuable tool for investors and traders alike. By using simulations, individuals can test out different strategies, analyze potential outcomes, and make more informed decisions when it comes to their investments.

In this chapter, we will explore the importance of simulating trading scenarios, the benefits of using simulation tools, and how to effectively use simulations to improve your trading strategy.

Why Simulate Trading Scenarios?

Simulating trading scenarios allows traders to test out different strategies in a risk-free environment. Instead of putting real money on the line, individuals can use simulation tools to see how their strategies would have performed in the past or how they might perform in the future.

By simulating different scenarios, traders can gain valuable insights into their trading strategy. They can identify potential weaknesses, test out new ideas, and make adjustments to their approach without risking any real capital.

In addition, simulating trading scenarios can help traders

build confidence in their strategy. By seeing positive results from their simulations, individuals can feel more comfortable implementing their strategy in real-world trading situations.

Benefits of Using Simulation Tools

There are several benefits to using simulation tools when it comes to trading scenarios. One of the main advantages is the ability to test out different strategies without any risk. By using a simulation tool, traders can see how their strategy would have performed in the past or how it might perform in the future.

Another benefit of using simulation tools is the ability to analyze potential outcomes. By running simulations, traders can see how different variables impact their strategy and make more informed decisions based on this information.

Simulation tools also allow traders to test out new ideas and make adjustments to their strategy. By experimenting with different scenarios, individuals can improve their trading approach and potentially increase their profits.

How to Use Simulations Effectively

To use simulations effectively, traders should follow a few key steps. First, individuals should clearly define their objectives and goals for the simulation. Whether they are testing out a new strategy or analyzing potential outcomes, having a clear goal in mind will help guide the simulation process.

Next, traders should carefully select the variables they want to test in the simulation. By focusing on specific variables, individuals can gain a better understanding of how these factors impact their strategy.

Once the simulation is set up, traders should analyze the results and draw conclusions based on the data. By reviewing the outcomes of the simulation, individuals can identify potential weaknesses in their strategy and make adjustments accordingly.

Overall, simulating trading scenarios can be a valuable tool for traders looking to improve their strategy and make more informed decisions. By using simulation tools, individuals can test out different strategies, analyze potential outcomes, and build confidence in their trading approach.

Simulating Various Market Conditions in python - scripts

Python is a powerful programming language that is widely used for data analysis, machine learning, and simulation. In this article, we will explore how to simulate various market conditions in Python using scripts.

Simulating market conditions can be useful for a variety of purposes, such as testing trading strategies, analyzing the impact of different factors on market prices, and predicting future market trends. By using Python scripts to simulate market conditions, we can easily manipulate different parameters and observe the resulting changes in market behavior.

To begin simulating market conditions in Python, we first need to define the basic components of a market simulation. These components include the market participants, the assets being traded, and the rules governing the trading activity.

Let's start by defining a simple market simulation with two types of market participants: buyers and sellers. We will also define a single asset that is being traded, such as a stock or a cryptocurrency. Finally, we will specify the rules for trading, such as the initial price of the asset, the trading volume, and the price changes over time.

```python
import random

class Market:
```

```python
def __init__(self, initial_price, trading_volume):
self.price = initial_price
self.volume = trading_volumeself.buyers = []
self.sellers = []

def add_buyer(self, buyer):self.buyers.append(buyer)

def add_seller(self, seller):self.sellers.append(seller)

def trade(self):
for buyer in self.buyers:
if buyer.price >= self.price: buyer.trade(self.price)
self.volume -= 1
self.price += 1
print("Buyer traded at price: ", self.price) for seller in self.sellers:
if seller.price <= self.price: seller.trade(self.price)
self.volume -= 1
self.price -= 1
print("Seller traded at price: ", self.price)


class Buyer:
def __init__(self, price):
self.price = price

def trade(self, price):
print("Buyer traded at price: ", price)

class Seller:
def __init__(self, price):
self.price = price
```

```
def trade(self, price):
print("Seller traded at price: ", price) market =
Market(100, 10)
for i in range(10):
buyer = Buyer(random.randint(90, 110)) seller =
Seller(random.randint(90, 110))market.add_buyer(buyer)
market.add_seller(seller)

market.trade()
```
```

In this script, we have defined a simple market simulation
with a single asset that starts at an initial price of 100 and
has a trading volume of 10. We then create 10 buyers and
sellers with random prices between 90 and 110 and add
them to the market. Finally, we simulate a trading session
where buyers and sellers trade based on the current
market price.

This is just a basic example of simulating market
conditions in Python. We can easily extend this script to
include more complex market dynamics, such as price
changes based on external factors, different types of
market participants, and more sophisticated trading
strategies.

For example, we can introduce a market maker who sets
the bid and ask prices based on the current market
conditions. We can also simulate the impact of news
events on market prices by incorporating a random factor
that influences price changes.

```python
```
```

```python
class MarketMaker:
    def __init__(self, bid_price, ask_price): self.bid_price = bid_price self.ask_price = ask_price

    def trade(self, market):
        if len(market.buyers) > len(market.sellers):

            self.ask_price += 1
        elif len(market.buyers) < len(market.sellers):
            self.bid_price -= 1
market_maker = MarketMaker(100, 100) for i in range(10):
    buyer = Buyer(random.randint(90, 110)) seller = Seller(random.randint(90, 110))market.add_buyer(buyer)
market.add_seller(seller)

market_maker.trade(market)market.trade()
```
```

In this extended script, we have introduced a market maker who adjusts the bid and ask prices based on the imbalance between buyers and sellers in the market. The market maker increases the ask price if there are more buyers than sellers, and decreases the bid price if there are more sellers than buyers.

By incorporating a market maker into our simulation, we can create a more realistic market environment where prices are influenced by the actions of market participants. This allows us to study the impact of liquidity providers on market prices and trading activity.
```

In addition to simulating market conditions with different types of market participants, we can also analyze the impact of different trading strategies on market performance. For example, we can create a simple trading strategy that buys

Evaluating Strategy Performance through Simulation in python – scripts

Simulation is a powerful tool that allows us to test and evaluate different strategies in a controlled environment. In this article, we will discuss how to evaluate strategy performance through simulation using Python scripts.

Python is a popular programming language that is widely used for data analysis, machine learning, and simulation. It provides a rich set of libraries and tools that make it easy to implement complex simulations and analyze the results.

To evaluate strategy performance through simulation, we first need to define our strategy and the rules that govern it. This could be a trading strategy, a marketing strategy, or any other type of strategy that we want to test.

Once we have defined our strategy, we can create a simulation environment in Python. This environment will simulate the behavior of the strategy over a specified period of time, taking into account factors such as market conditions, competition, and random events.

To illustrate this process, let's consider a simple trading strategy that buys a stock when its price crosses above a moving average and sells it when the price crosses below the moving average. We will use Python to implement this strategy and evaluate its performance through simulation.

First, we need to import the necessary libraries in Python:

```python
import numpy as np
import pandas as pd
import matplotlib.pyplot as plt
```

Next, we will define our trading strategy:

```python
def moving_average_strategy(data, window):
    signals = pd.DataFrame(index=data.index)
    signals['price'] = data['price']
    signals['moving_average'] = data['price'].rolling(window=window).mean()
    signals['position'] = np.where(signals['price'] > signals['moving_average'], 1, -1)
    signals['position'] = signals['position'].shift(1)
    signals['strategy_return'] = signals['position'] * signals['price'].pct_change()
    return signals
```

In this function, we calculate the moving average of the stock price over a specified window and generate buy/sell signals based on the crossing of the price and the moving average. We then calculate the strategy return based on the position and the price change.

Next, we will create a simulation environment to test our strategy:

```python
def simulate_strategy(data, window):
    signals = moving_average_strategy(data, window)
    signals.dropna(inplace=True)
    signals['cumulative_return'] = (1 + signals['strategy_return']).cumprod()return signals
```

In this function, we apply the trading strategy to the historical stock price data and calculate the cumulative return of the strategy over time.

Finally, we can visualize the performance of our strategy through simulation:

```python
data = pd.read_csv('stock_price_data.csv')
data.set_index('date', inplace=True)

window = 50
signals = simulate_strategy(data, window)

plt.figure(figsize=(10, 6))    plt.plot(signals['price'], label='Price')
plt.plot(signals['moving_average'], label='Moving Average')
plt.legend()
plt.show()

plt.figure(figsize=(10, 6))
plt.plot(signals['cumulative_return'], label='Cumulative
```

```
Return') plt.legend()
plt.show()
```

In this example, we load historical stock price data from a CSV file, apply the moving average trading strategy with a window of 50 days, and visualize the stock price, moving average, and cumulative return of the strategy.

By running this script in Python, we can evaluate the performance of our trading strategy through simulation and analyze the results to determine its effectiveness.

evaluating strategy performance through simulation in Python is a powerful technique that allows us to test and optimize different strategies in a controlled environment.

By defining our strategy, creating a simulation environment, and analyzing the results, we can gain valuable insights into the effectiveness of our strategies and make informed decisions to improve their performance. Python provides a flexible and efficient platform for implementing simulations and analyzing the results, making it an ideal choice for evaluating strategy performance in a variety of domains.

Chapter 20: Paper Trading vs. Live Trading

When it comes to trading in the financial markets, there are two main ways to practice and execute trades: paper trading and live trading. Both methods have their own advantages and disadvantages, and it is important for traders to understand the differences between the two in order to make informed decisions about how to approach their trading activities.

Paper trading, also known as simulated trading or demo trading, is a practice in which traders use a simulated trading platform to execute trades without using real money. This allows traders to test out different trading strategies, practice their skills, and gain experience in the markets without risking any capital. Paper trading is often used by beginner traders as a way to learn the basics of trading before transitioning to live trading.

One of the main advantages of paper trading is that it allows traders to gain experience in the markets without the risk of losing money. This can be especially beneficial for beginner traders who are still learning the ropes and may not have a lot of capital to risk. Paper trading also allows traders to test out different trading strategies and techniques to see what works best for them before risking real money.

However, there are also some drawbacks to paper trading. One of the main disadvantages is that it does not fully replicate the experience of live trading. In paper trading, there is no emotional attachment to the trades since no real money is at stake, which can lead to a lack of discipline and unrealistic expectations. Additionally, paper trading does not account for factors such as slippage, market liquidity, and other real-world conditions that can impact trading performance.

On the other hand, live trading involves executing trades with real money in the financial markets. Live trading requires traders to have a capital stake in the trades they make, which can lead to both profits and losses. Live trading is the ultimate test of a trader's skills and abilities, as it requires them to make decisions under real market conditions and deal with the emotional aspects of trading.

One of the main advantages of live trading is that it provides a more realistic trading experience compared to paper trading. Traders are able to experience the highs and lows of trading with real money on the line, which can help them develop the discipline and emotional control needed to be successful in the markets. Live trading also allows traders to take advantage of opportunities in the markets and potentially earn profits from their trades.

However, live trading also comes with its own set of challenges and risks. One of the main disadvantages of live trading is the potential for significant losses. Since real money is at stake, traders can experience financial losses if their trades do not go as planned. Live trading also requires traders to manage their emotions and avoid making impulsive decisions that can lead to losses.

Both paper trading and live trading have their own advantages and disadvantages. Paper trading is a useful tool for beginner traders to practice their skills and test out different strategies without risking real money. Live trading, on the other hand, provides a more realistic trading experience and allows traders to potentially earn profits from their trades. Ultimately, the choice between paper trading and live trading will depend on the individual trader's goals, risk tolerance, and level of experience in the markets.

Differences and Transition Strategies in Trading

Trading in financial markets can be a lucrative venture for those who are able to navigate the complexities of the market effectively. However, trading in different languages can present unique challenges that traders must be aware of in order to be successful. In this article, we will explore the differences and transition strategies in trading in different languages.

One of the main differences in trading in different languages is the language barrier itself. While English is widely spoken and understood in the financial markets, there are still many traders who prefer to conduct their transactions in their native language. This can create challenges for traders who are not fluent in the language that is being used, as they may struggle to understand market news, analysis, and other important information that is being communicated in that language.

Another key difference in trading in different languages is the cultural differences that can impact trading practices. Different cultures have different attitudes towards risk, money, and investing, which can influence trading decisions and strategies. Traders who are not familiar with the cultural nuances of the language that they are trading in may struggle to understand the motivations behind certain trading behaviors, which can impact their ability to make informed decisions.

In order to successfully transition into trading in a different language, traders must be aware of these differences and develop strategies to overcome them. One strategy that traders can use is to immerse themselves in the language and culture of the market that they are trading in. This can involve taking language classes, reading market news and analysis in the target language, and engaging with native speakers to gain a better understandingof the nuances of the language and culture.

Traders can also use translation tools and services to help bridge the language gap. There are many online tools and services that can help traders translate market news, analysis, and other important information into their native language, making it easier for them to stay informed and make informed trading decisions.

Another important strategy for transitioning into trading in a different language is to build a network of contacts in the target market. By connecting with native speakers, other traders, and industry professionals in the target market, traders can gain valuable insights into the market dynamics, trading practices, and cultural nuances that can impact their trading decisions.

It is also important for traders to be patient and persistent when transitioning into trading in a different language. Learning a new language and understanding a new culture takes time and effort, and traders must be willing to put in the work in order to be successful. By staying committed to their language and cultural studies, traders can overcome the challenges of trading in a different language and position themselves for success in the target market.

Trading in different languages presents unique challenges

that traders must be aware of in order to be successful. By understanding the differences in language and culture, and developing strategies to overcome them, traders can successfully transition into trading in a different language and position themselves for success in the target market. With patience, persistence, and a commitment to learning, traders can overcome the challenges of trading in different languages and thrive in the global financial markets.

Implementing Paper Trading Systems in Python - scripts

Paper trading systems are a great way for traders to practice their strategies and test out new ideas without risking real money. By using simulated trading environments, traders can gain valuable experience and confidence before committing their funds to the market. In this article, we will discuss how to implement paper trading systems in Python, with example scripts to help you get started.

Python is a popular programming language among traders and developers due to its simplicity and versatility. It offers a wide range of libraries and tools that make it easy to build complex trading systems. In this guide, we will use Python to create a paper trading system that simulates buying and selling assets based on predefined rules.

To get started, you will need to install Python on your computer. You can download the latest version of Python from the official website and follow the installation instructions. Once you have Python installed, you can start writing your paper trading scripts.

The first step in creating a paper trading system is to define the rules for buying and selling assets. This can be based on technical indicators, fundamental analysis, or any other criteria that you choose. For this example, we will create a simple moving average crossover strategy.

In a moving average crossover strategy, we will buy an

asset when its short-term moving average crosses above its long-term moving average, and sell when the short-term moving average crosses below the long-term moving average. This is a popular strategy among traders and can be easily implemented in Python.

To implement this strategy, we will first need to import the necessary libraries. We will use the pandas library to handle data manipulation and the matplotlib library to visualize our trading signals. You can install these libraries using the pip package manager by running the following commands in your terminal:

```
pip install pandas pip install matplotlib
```

Next, we will define a function that generates random price data for our paper trading system. This function will create a DataFrame with random prices for a given number of days. We will use this function to simulate the price data for our assets.

```python
import pandas as pd import numpy as np

def generate_price_data(days):
dates = pd.date_range(start='1/1/2022', periods=days)
prices = np.random.randint(1, 100, size=days)

return pd.DataFrame({'Date': dates, 'Price': prices})
```

Now that we have our price data, we can implement the

227

moving average crossover strategy. We will define a function that calculates the short-term and long-term moving averages for our asset prices and generates buy andsell signals based on the crossover.

```python
def moving_average_crossover(data,    short_window=5, long_window=20):
data['Short_MA']                       =
data['Price'].rolling(window=short_window).mean()
data['Long_MA']                        =
data['Price'].rolling(window=long_window).mean()

data['Signal'] = 0
data['Signal'][short_window:]          =
np.where(data['Short_MA'][short_window:]        >
data['Long_MA'][short_window:], 1, 0)
data['Position'] = data['Signal'].diff()

return data
```

In this function, we calculate the short-term and long-term moving averages using the rolling() method from the pandas library. We then generate buy and sell signals based on the crossover of the moving averages. A buy signal is generated when the short-term moving average crosses above the long-term moving average, and a sell signal is generated when the short-term moving average crosses below the long-term moving average.

Finally, we can test our paper trading system by running the following script:

```python
price_data = generate_price_data(100)
signals = moving_average_crossover(price_data)

plt.figure(figsize=(10,5))
plt.plot(price_data['Date'],                price_data['Price'],
label='Price')                  plt.plot(price_data['Date'],
price_data['Short_MA'],          label='Short          MA')
plt.plot(price_data['Date'],         price_data['Long_MA'],
label='Long MA')
plt.plot(price_data['Date'],               signals['Signal']*100,
label='Signal', marker='o', linestyle='')plt.legend()
plt.show()
```

This script will generate random price data for 100 days, calculate the moving averages, and plot the price data along with the buy and sell signals. You can customize the parameters of the moving average crossover strategy by changing the short_window and long_window variables.

Paper trading systems are a valuable tool for traders to test their strategies and improve their skills. By implementing a paper trading system in Python, you can simulate trading scenarios and evaluate the performance of your strategies without risking real money. The example scripts provided in this guide will help you get started with building your paper trading system in Python.

In addition to the moving average crossover strategy, you can explore other trading strategies and indicators to enhance your paper trading system. Python offers a wide range of libraries and tools that make it easy

Chapter 21: Real-Time Trading Execution

In the fast-paced world of trading, every second counts. Real-time trading execution is crucial for traders looking to make split-second decisions and capitalize on market opportunities. In this chapter, we will explore the importance of real-time trading execution, the technology behind it, and best practices for successful execution.

Real-time trading execution refers to the process of executing trades instantaneously as market conditions change. This requires traders to have access to up-to-date market data, advanced trading platforms, and high-speed connectivity to ensure that trades are executed quickly and accurately.

One of the key benefits of real-time trading execution is the ability to react quickly to market movements. By monitoring market data in real-time, traders can make informed decisions and execute trades at the optimal time. This can help traders take advantage of short-term opportunities and maximize profits.

Another benefit of real-time trading execution is the ability to manage risk effectively. By executing trades quickly, traders can limit their exposure to market fluctuations and reduce the impact of sudden price changes. This can help traders protect their capital and minimize losses.

Real-time trading execution is made possible by advanced trading technology, including high-speed trading platforms, algorithmic trading systems, and direct market access (DMA) tools. These technologies allow traders to access market data, execute trades, and manage risk with speed and precision.

High-speed trading platforms are essential for real-time trading execution. These platforms provide traders with real-time market data, advanced charting tools, and order execution capabilities. By using a high-speed trading platform, traders can react quickly to market movements and execute trades with minimal latency.

Algorithmic trading systems are another key technology for real-time trading execution. These systems use complex algorithms to analyze market data, identify trading opportunities, and execute trades automatically. By using algorithmic trading systems, traders can execute trades at high speeds and take advantage of market inefficiencies.

Direct market access (DMA) tools are also important for real-time trading execution. DMA tools allow traders to access liquidity directly from exchanges and execute trades without the need for a broker. This can help traders reduce trading costs, minimize latency, and improve execution quality.

In addition to advanced trading technology, successful real-time trading execution requires traders to follow best practices. These include:

Stay informed: Keep up-to-date with market news, economic data, and company announcements to make informed trading decisions.

Use stop-loss orders: Set stop-loss orders to limit losses and protect your capital in case of adverse market movements.

Diversify your portfolio: Spread your investments across different asset classes, sectors, and regions to reduce risk and maximize returns.

Practice risk management: Use proper risk management techniques, such as position sizing and leverage control, to protect your capital and manage risk effectively.

Monitor your trades: Keep track of your open positions, monitor market movements, and adjust your trading strategy as needed to optimize performance.

By following these best practices and leveraging advanced trading technology, traders can improve their real- time trading execution and achieve better results in today's fast-paced markets.

Real-time trading execution is essential for traders looking to capitalize on market opportunities and manage risk effectively. By using advanced trading technology, following best practices, and staying informed, traders can execute trades quickly and accurately to achieve their trading goals. With the right tools and strategies, traders can navigate the complexities of real-time trading execution and succeed in today's dynamic markets.

Managing Real-Time Data and Orders in Trading

Managing real-time data and orders in trading is crucial for traders to make informed decisions and execute trades effectively. In today's fast-paced and volatile markets, having access to real-time data and the ability to place orders quickly is essential for success. In this article, we will discuss the importance of managing real-time data and orders in trading, as well as some best practices for doing so.

Real-time data refers to the most up-to-date information available on a particular asset or market. This data includes price quotes, volume, bid and ask sizes, and other relevant information that can help traders make informed decisions. In the world of trading, where prices can change rapidly and unexpectedly, having access to real-time data is crucial for staying ahead of the market and making profitable trades.

One of the key challenges in managing real-time data is the sheer volume of information that traders need to process. With thousands of assets and markets to monitor, traders can quickly become overwhelmed by the sheer volume of data available. This is where technology can help. By using advanced trading platforms and software, traders can automate the process of collecting, analyzing, and displaying real-time data, making it easier to stay on top of market movements and make quick decisions.

In addition to managing real-time data, traders also need to effectively manage their orders. Placing orders quickly and accurately is essential for executing trades at the desired price and time. Failing to manage orders effectively can result in missed opportunities, slippage, and other costly mistakes. To avoid these pitfalls, traders need to have a well-defined order management strategy in place.

One important aspect of order management is setting clear entry and exit points for each trade. By establishing specific price levels at which to enter and exit a trade, traders can minimize their risk and maximize their potential profits. This requires careful analysis of market trends, as well as a solid understanding of technical and fundamental analysis techniques.

Another key aspect of order management is using stop-loss and take-profit orders to manage risk and protect profits. Stop-loss orders automatically close a trade when the price reaches a certain level, limiting the trader's losses. Take-profit orders, on the other hand, automatically close a trade when the price reaches a specified profit target, locking in gains. By using these types of orders, traders can effectively manage their risk and ensure that they do not let their emotions dictate their trading decisions.

In addition to setting clear entry and exit points, traders also need to monitor their orders in real-time to ensure that they are being executed as intended. This requires constant vigilance and the ability to react quickly to changing market conditions. By staying on top of their orders and adjusting them as needed, traders can minimize their risk and maximize their profits.

One of the best ways to manage real-time data and orders in trading is to use a reliable and user-friendly trading platform. There are many different trading platforms available, each with its own set of features and capabilities. When choosing a trading platform, traders should look for one that offers real-time data feeds, advanced charting tools, order management capabilities, and other useful features.

Some popular trading platforms that offer real-time data and order management capabilities include MetaTrader, NinjaTrader, and Thinkorswim. These platforms are widely used by traders around the world and are known for their reliability, speed, and ease of use. By using a reputable trading platform, traders can streamline the process of managing real-time data and orders, making it easier to stay on top of market movements and execute trades effectively.

Managing real-time data and orders in trading is essential for success in today's fast-paced and volatile markets. By having access to up-to-date information and the ability to place orders quickly and accurately, traders can make informed decisions and execute profitable trades.

By following best practices for managing real-time data and orders, traders can minimize their risk, protect their profits, and stay ahead of the market. By using a reliable trading platform and staying on top of market trends, traders can increase their chances of success and achieve their trading goals.

Implementing Execution Algorithms in Python - scripts

Execution algorithms are an essential part of programming, as they determine the order in which instructions are executed by a computer. In Python, there are various ways to implement execution algorithms, such as using scripts. In this article, we will explore how to implement execution algorithms in Python using scripts, with examples to demonstrate their functionality.

One common execution algorithm is the sequential execution, where instructions are executed in a linear order from top to bottom. This is the default behavior in most programming languages, including Python. Here is an example of a simple script that demonstrates sequential execution:

```python
# Sequential execution exampleprint("Hello,")
print("world!")
```

When you run this script, the output will be:

```
Hello,world!
```

As you can see, the instructions in the script are executed sequentially, with the `print("Hello,")` statement executed first, followed by the `print("world!")` statement.

Another common execution algorithm is the conditional execution, where instructions are executed based on certain conditions. In Python, conditional execution is implemented using if-else statements. Here is an example of a script that demonstrates conditional execution:

```python
# Conditional execution examplex = 10

if x > 5:
print("x is greater than 5")else:
print("x is less than or equal to 5")
```

When you run this script with `x = 10`, the output will be:

```
x is greater than 5
```

In this example, the `if x > 5` condition is true, so the `print("x is greater than 5")` statement is executed. If you change the value of `x` to 3 and run the script again, the output will be:

```
x is less than or equal to 5
```

In this case, the `if x > 5` condition is false, so the `print("x is less than or equal to 5")` statement is executed instead.

Another important execution algorithm is the iterative execution, where instructions are executed repeatedly until a certain condition is met. In Python, iterative execution is implemented using loops. Here is an example of a script that demonstrates iterative execution using a while loop:

```python
# Iterative execution examplex = 0

while x < 5:
print(x)x += 1
```

When you run this script, the output will be:

```
0
1
2
3
4
```

In this example, the `while x < 5` condition is true, so the `print(x)` statement is executed repeatedly until `x` is no longer less than 5.

These are just a few examples of how execution algorithms can be implemented in Python using scripts. By combining sequential, conditional, and iterative execution, you can create complex programs that perform a wide range of tasks. Experiment with different algorithms and see how they affect the behavior of your scripts. Happy coding!

Chapter 22: Building a Trading Dashboard in python

In this chapter, we will learn how to build a trading dashboard in Python using various libraries and tools. A trading dashboard is a visual representation of various data points related to trading activities, such as stock prices, volume, and indicators. By creating a trading dashboard, traders can easily monitor and analyze market trends and make informed decisions.

To build a trading dashboard in Python, we will use the following libraries:

Pandas: Pandas is a powerful data manipulation library that provides data structures and functions for working with structured data.

Matplotlib: Matplotlib is a plotting library that allows us to create various types of charts and graphs, such as line charts, bar charts, and scatter plots.

Plotly: Plotly is an interactive plotting library that allows us to create interactive and customizable charts and graphs.

Dash: Dash is a web application framework that allows us to create interactive web applications with Python.

To start building our trading dashboard, we first need to collect and process the data. We can use the Pandas library to read data from various sources, such as CSV files, APIs, or databases. Once we have the data, we can use Pandas to clean, manipulate, and analyze the data.

Next, we can use Matplotlib and Plotly to create various charts and graphs to visualize the data. For example, we can create a line chart to show the historical stock prices, a bar chart to show the trading volume, and a scatter plot to show the correlation between different variables.

After creating the charts and graphs, we can use Dash to create an interactive web application that displays the trading dashboard. With Dash, we can add interactive elements, such as dropdown menus, sliders, and buttons, to allow users to customize the dashboard and explore the data in more detail.

In addition to displaying historical data, we can also add real-time data updates to the trading dashboard. We can use APIs to fetch real-time data, such as stock prices and news articles, and update the dashboard dynamically.

Overall, building a trading dashboard in Python can help traders to monitor market trends, analyze trading activities, and make informed decisions. By using libraries such as Pandas, Matplotlib, Plotly, and Dash, we can create a powerful and interactive dashboard that provides valuable insights for traders.

Designing and Developing a Trading Dashboard in python

A trading dashboard is a crucial tool for traders to monitor and analyze their trading activities. It provides a comprehensive overview of the market, including real-time data, charts, and indicators. In this article, we will discuss how to design and develop a trading dashboard in Python.

To create a trading dashboard, we will use Python's popular libraries such as Pandas, Matplotlib, and Plotly. These libraries will help us to fetch data from various sources, visualize the data, and create interactive charts for better analysis.

First, we need to set up our development environment by installing the necessary libraries. You can install the libraries using the following commands:

```
```

pip install pandas pip install matplotlibpip install plotly
```
```

Once the libraries are installed, we can start designing the trading dashboard. The first step is to fetch data from a source like a CSV file or an API. For this example, let's assume we have a CSV file containing historical stock price data.

We can use Pandas to read the CSV file and load the data into a DataFrame. Here is an example code snippet to read the CSV file:

```python
import pandas as pd

data = pd.read_csv('stock_data.csv')
```

Next, we can use Matplotlib to create a simple line chart to visualize the stock price data. Here is an example code snippet to create a line chart:

```python
import matplotlib.pyplot as plt

plt.plot(data['Date'], data['Close'])plt.xlabel('Date')
plt.ylabel('Close Price') plt.title('Stock Price Chart')
plt.show()
```

The line chart will display the stock's closing price over time, providing a visual representation of the stock's performance.

To make the trading dashboard more interactive, we can use Plotly to create interactive charts. Plotly allows us to create interactive plots that can be customized and manipulated by users. Here is an example code snippet to create an interactive line chart using Plotly:

```python
import plotly.express as px
```

244

```python
fig = px.line(data, x='Date', y='Close', title='Stock Price Chart')fig.show()
```

The interactive line chart will allow users to zoom in, zoom out, and hover over data points to view detailed information.

In addition to visualizing stock price data, a trading dashboard should also include key performance indicators (KPIs) such as moving averages, relative strength index (RSI), and moving average convergence divergence (MACD). These indicators help traders to make informed decisions based on technical analysis.

We can calculate these indicators using Pandas and add them to the trading dashboard. Here is an example code snippet to calculate the 50-day moving average and add it to the DataFrame:

```python
data['MA50'] = data['Close'].rolling(window=50).mean()
```

We can then plot the moving average on the line chart using Matplotlib or Plotly.

Similarly, we can calculate other indicators like RSI and MACD and add them to the trading dashboard. Here is an example code snippet to calculate the RSI and MACD:

```python
```

```
data['RSI'] = calculate_rsi(data['Close']) data['MACD'] =
calculate_macd(data['Close'])
```

The `calculate_rsi` and `calculate_macd` functions can be implemented using technical analysis formulas. Once the indicators are calculated, we can add them to the trading dashboard for better analysis.

In addition to visualizing stock price data and technical indicators, a trading dashboard should also include features like news feeds, economic calendars, and watchlists. These features provide traders with valuable information to make informed decisions.

We can use APIs to fetch news articles and economic data and display them on the trading dashboard. For example, we can use the News API to fetch the latest news articles related to a specific stock and display them on the dashboard.

```python
import requests

url = 'https://newsapi.org/v2/everything'
params = {
'q': 'AAPL',
'apiKey': 'YOUR_API_KEY'
}

response = requests.get(url, params=params)
news = response.json()

for article in news['articles']:
print(article['title'])
```

We can also use APIs like the Investing.com API to fetch economic data such as economic indicators, earnings calendar, and economic news. By integrating these features into the trading dashboard, traders can stay informed about market events and make better trading decisions.

Designing and developing a trading dashboard in Python involves fetching data, visualizing data, calculating technical indicators, and integrating features like news feeds and economic calendars. By using libraries like Pandas, Matplotlib, and Plotly, traders can create a comprehensive dashboard to monitor and analyze their trading activities effectively.

Integrating Performance Metrics and Alerts in python - scripts

Performance metrics and alerts are essential components of any software application or system. They help in monitoring the performance of the application in real-time and alerting the stakeholders about any potential issues or bottlenecks. In this article, we will discuss how to integrate performance metrics and alerts in Python using scripts as an example.

Performance metrics are quantitative measures that help in evaluating the performance of a system or application. These metrics can include response time, throughput, error rate, and resource utilization. By monitoring these metrics, developers and operators can identify performance issues, bottlenecks, and areas for improvement.

Alerts, on the other hand, are notifications that are triggered when certain predefined conditions are met. These conditions can be based on performance metrics, such as response time exceeding a certain threshold or error rate exceeding a certain percentage. Alerts help in proactively identifying and addressing performance issues before they impact the end-users.

Integrating performance metrics and alerts in Python can be achieved using various libraries and tools. One popular library for monitoring performance metrics is Prometheus, which provides a flexible and scalable platform for collecting and querying metrics. For alerting, tools like Prometheus Alertmanager can be used to define and manage alerting rules.

Let's consider an example where we have a Python application that serves HTTP requests. We want to monitor the response time of the application and trigger an alert if the response time exceeds a certain threshold. We will use Prometheus for collecting metrics and Alertmanager for defining alerting rules.

First, we need to instrument our Python application to expose performance metrics. We can use the Prometheus client library for Python to do this. Here is an example of how we can instrument our application to expose response time metrics:

```python
from prometheus_client import start_http_server, Summaryimport random
import time

# Create a metric to track response time
REQUEST_TIME                              =
Summary('request_processing_seconds',  'Time  spent
processing request')

#      Decorate      function      with      metric
@REQUEST_TIME.time()
def process_request():
# Simulate processing time time.sleep(random.random())

if____name_== '__main_':
#    Start    HTTP    server    to    expose    metrics
```

```
start_http_server(8000)
```

```
# Process requests indefinitelywhile True:
process_request()
```

In this script, we have defined a `REQUEST_TIME`
metric using the `Summary` class from the Prometheus
client library. We have also decorated the
`process_request` function with the
`REQUEST_TIME.time()` decorator to track the response
time of the function. The `start_http_server(8000)` call
starts an HTTP server onport 8000 to expose the metrics.

Next, we need to configure Prometheus to scrape the
metrics from our Python application. We can do this by
adding a job configuration to the Prometheus
configuration file:

```yaml
scrape_configs:
job_name: 'python-app'static_configs:
targets: ['localhost:8000']
```

This configuration tells Prometheus to scrape metrics from
the Python application runningon `localhost:8000`.

Now that we have configured Prometheus to collect
metrics from our Python application, we can define
alerting rules using Alertmanager. Here is an example of
an alerting rule that triggers an alert if the response time
exceeds 1 second:

```yaml
groups:
name: examplerules:
```

```
alert: HighResponseTime
expr:          request_processing_seconds_sum          /
request_processing_seconds_count  > 1for: 1m
labels:
severity: warning annotations:
summary: High response time detected
```

This rule defines an alert named `HighResponseTime` that triggers when the average response time exceeds 1 second for a period of 1 minute. The alert has a severity of `warning` and a summary message of `High response time detected`.

Finally, we need to configure Alertmanager to send notifications when alerts are triggered. We can do this by adding a notification configuration to the Alertmanager configuration file:

```yaml
route:
group_by: ['alertname'] group_wait: 10s group_interval:
5m repeat_interval: 3h routes:
receiver: 'email'match:
severity: warning routes:
match_re:
alertname: HighResponseTime receiver: 'slack'

receivers:
name: 'email' email_configs:
to: 'admin@example.com'

name: 'slack' slack_configs:
```

```
api_url:
'https://hooks.slack.com/services/T00000000/B00000000
/XXXXXXXXXXXXXXXXXXXXXXXX'
```

This configuration tells Alertmanager to send email notifications to `admin@example.com` for alerts with a severity of `warning` and to send Slack notifications to a Slack channel using a webhook URL for the `HighResponseTime` alert.

Conclusion

As we reach the end of *"Python for Algorithmic Trading: Mastering Strategies for Consistent Profits"*, you are now equipped with a comprehensive toolkit to navigate the intricate world of algorithmic trading. This book has taken you on a detailed journey, providing step-by-step guidance on creating and implementing robust trading strategies using Python.

Throughout these chapters, we've delved into the essentials of algorithmic trading, from understanding market dynamics and data preprocessing to deploying sophisticated machine learning models and backtesting your strategies. Each section has been crafted to empower you with practical skills and knowledge, enabling you to transform raw data into actionable trading insights.

The core message of this book is clear: Mastery of algorithmic trading requires both technical expertise and strategic acumen. By leveraging the power of Python, you can enhance your trading efficiency, reduce the risks associated with manual trading, and ultimately boost your profitability. The strategies and techniques you've learned are not just theoretical concepts—they are practical tools designed to help you succeed in the fast-paced, ever-evolving financial markets.

But remember, the journey doesn't end here. Algorithmic trading is a dynamic field that demands continuous learning and adaptation. As market conditions change and new technologies emerge, staying ahead of the curve will require ongoing effort and innovation. Use the foundations laid in this book as a springboard for further exploration and development.

Biography

J.P. Morgan is a distinguished expert in the realm of algorithmic trading, blending a profound knowledge of finance with a mastery of Python programming. With a passion for unlocking the potential of data-driven strategies, J.P. Morgan has dedicated their career to transforming the complexities of trading into actionable insights and consistent profits.

J.P. Morgan's journey in the financial world began with a robust academic foundation in finance and computer science. This unique blend of disciplines has equipped them with the analytical skills and technical acumen required to excel in algorithmic trading. Over the years, they have honed their expertise, developing and implementing sophisticated trading algorithms that navigate the dynamic landscape of the financial markets with precision and efficiency.

In addition to their professional achievements, J.P. Morgan is an avid Python enthusiast and web development aficionado. Their deep-seated interest in technology drives their continuous exploration of innovative solutions to enhance trading strategies and performance. Outside of the trading floor, J.P. Morgan enjoys sharing their knowledge through writing, teaching, and mentoring aspiring traders and programmers.

J.P. Morgan's dedication to education and empowerment is evident in their writing. In *Python for Algorithmic Trading: Mastering Strategies for Consistent Profits*, they combine their extensive experience with a passion for teaching, providing readers with a comprehensive guide to algorithmic trading. Their approachable style and practical insights make complex concepts accessible, inspiring readers to harness the power of Python to achieve their trading goals.

Glossary: Python for Algorithmic Trading

Python is a high-level programming language that has gained immense popularity in the field of algorithmic trading. It is known for its simplicity, readability, and versatility, making it an ideal choice for developing trading strategies and implementing quantitative analysis in financial markets. In this glossary, we will explore some of the key terms and concepts related to Python in the context of algorithmic trading.

Algorithmic Trading: Algorithmic trading refers to the use of computer algorithms to execute trading strategies in financial markets. These algorithms can analyze market data, identify trading opportunities, and automatically place trades based on predefined rules. Python is a popular programming language for developing algorithmic trading strategies due to its ease of use and extensive libraries for data analysis and visualization.

Backtesting: Backtesting is the process of testing a trading strategy on historical market data to evaluate its performance. Python provides tools and libraries for backtesting trading strategies, allowing traders to assess the profitability and risk of their strategies before deploying them in live markets.

Data Analysis: Data analysis involves processing and analyzing large datasets to extract valuable insights for decision-making. Python's libraries, such as Pandas and NumPy, are widely used for data analysis in algorithmic trading. These libraries provide powerful tools for manipulating data, performing statistical analysis, and visualizing results.

Machine Learning: Machine learning is a branch of artificial intelligence that involves developing algorithms that can learn from data and make predictions or decisions. Python's libraries, such as scikit-learn and TensorFlow, are popular choices for implementing machine learning models in algorithmic trading. These libraries provide tools for training and testing models, as well as for evaluating their performance.

Quantitative Analysis: Quantitative analysis involves using mathematical and statistical techniques to analyze financial data and make informed trading decisions. Python's libraries, such as QuantLib and StatsModels, provide tools for performing quantitative analysis in algorithmic trading. These libraries offer functions for calculating risk metrics, estimating asset prices, and testing trading strategies.

Risk Management: Risk management is the process of identifying, assessing, and mitigating risks in trading activities. Python's libraries, such as Pyfolio and Riskfolio, provide tools for measuring and managing risk in algorithmic trading. These libraries offer functions for calculating risk metrics, optimizing portfolio allocations, and monitoring risk exposure.

Trading Platform: A trading platform is a software application that allows traders to execute trades, monitor market data, and analyze trading performance. Python can be used to develop custom trading platforms for algorithmic trading. Traders can leverage Python's libraries and frameworks, such as Flask and Django, to build interactive and user-friendly trading platforms.

API Integration: API integration involves connecting trading platforms with external data sources, such as market data feeds and brokerages. Python's libraries, such as requests and websocket-client, provide tools for integrating APIs in algorithmic trading. Traders can use Python to retrieve real-time market data, place trades, and manage accounts through API connections.

Event-Driven Programming: Event-driven programming is a programming paradigm that involves responding to events or signals in real-time. Python's libraries, such as asyncio and Twisted, support event-driven programming for algorithmic trading. Traders can use Python to build event-driven systems that react to market events and execute trading strategies accordingly.

Optimization: Optimization involves finding the best set of parameters or variables to maximize a trading strategy's performance. Python's libraries, such as scipy.optimize and cvxpy, provide tools for optimizing trading strategies in algorithmic trading. These libraries offer functions for solving optimization problems, such as portfolio allocation and risk management.

Portfolio Management: Portfolio management involves selecting and managing a collection of assets to achieve investment objectives. Python's libraries, such as PyPortfolioOpt and PortfolioAnalytics, provide tools for optimizing portfolio allocations in algorithmic trading. Traders can use Python to build diversified portfolios, rebalance asset allocations, and monitor portfolio performance.

Technical Analysis: Technical analysis involves analyzing historical price data and trading volumes to forecast future price movements. Python's libraries, such as TA-Lib and mplfinance, provide tools for performing technical analysis in algorithmic trading. These libraries offer functions for calculating technical indicators, plotting price charts, and identifying trading signals.

Simulation: Simulation involves replicating real-world market conditions in a controlled environment to test trading strategies. Python's libraries, such as simpy and backtrader, provide tools for simulating trading strategies in algorithmic trading. Traders can use Python to run simulations, analyze results, and optimize trading strategiesbefore deploying them in live markets.

Statistical Arbitrage: Statistical arbitrage is a trading strategy that involves exploiting price discrepancies between related assets. Python's libraries, such as statsmodels and scipy, provide tools for implementing statistical arbitrage strategies in algorithmic trading. Traders can use Python to identify cointegrated pairs, calculate spread ratios, and execute arbitrage trades.

Time Series Analysis: Time series analysis involves analyzing sequential data points to identify patterns and trends over time.

www.ingramcontent.com/pod-product-compliance
Lightning Source LLC
LaVergne TN
LVHW051441050326
832903LV00030BD/3190

* 9 7 9 8 3 3 5 1 7 8 2 3 5 *